# ANECDOTES OF AURANGZIB

# ANECDOTES OF AURANGZIB

**(English translation of AHKAM-I-ALAMGIRI ascribed to Hamid-ud-din Khan Bahadur)**

WITH

**A Life of Aurangzib and Historical Notes**

**JADUNATH SARKAR, M.A.**

**SECOND EDITION REVISED**

GYAN

*Published by*

GYAN

Gyan Publishing House
5, Ansari Road
Daryaganj, New Delhi-110002
Phone: 011-47034999, 9811692060
E-mail: books@gyanbooks.com

*Distribution Network*
gyanbooks.com
India, USA, Canada, UK, Australia, France



ISBN : 978-81-212-6717-5 (PB)
First Published, 1925

2nd Impression 2022

*Printed at:* Gyan Press, Delhi.



**ANECDOTES OF AURANGZIB**
Author: JADUNATH SARKAR

# ANECDOTES OF AURANGZIB

(English translation of **AHKAM-I-ALAMGIRI** ascribed to Hamid-ud-din Khan Bahadur)

WITH

## A Life of Aurangzib and Historical Notes

JADUNATH SARKAR, M.A.,
*Indian Educational Service.*

SECOND EDITION, REVISED

1925

*Bibliographical Note.*—The English translation of these anecdotes was first printed by me in 1912 and issued bound up with the short life of Aurangzib and ten essays as *Anecdotes of Aurangzib and Historical Essays.* The same impression of the translation and life was also issued bound up with the Persian text as *Ahkam-i-Alamgiri,* in 1915. In the second edition the Persian text, translation, and essays have been completely separated, with the respective titles of *Ahkam-i-Alamgiri* (1925), *Anecdotes of Aurangzib* (1925), and *Studies in Mughal India* (1919), the life of Aurangzib alone being common to the second and third of these works, and *twelve* new essays added to the last. The Persian text and translation have been minutely revised and corrected and much new information added in the notes, in preparing the second edition, while the short life of Aurangzib in its present form has been improved by incorporation of facts from my longer *History of Aurangzib* in five volumes now completed (in 1924). In the first edition of the Persian *Ahkam* many misprints occurred through the negligence of the press. These have been now removed, and in several cases also a different reading of the MS. has been accepted by me as the result of reconsideration and thirteen years' further study.

J. SARKAR,
*July, 1925.*

# LIFE OF AURANGZIB

## EARLY LIFE

MUHI-UD-DIN Muhammad Aurangzib, the third son of the Emperor Shah Jahan and his famous consort Mumtaz Mahal, was born on 24th October, 1618, at Dohad, now a town in the Panch Mahal *taluq* of the Bombay Presidency and a station on the Godra-Rutlam railway line. The most notable incident of his boyhood was his display of cool courage when charged by an infuriated elephant during an elephant combat under his father's eyes on the bank of the Jamuna outside Agra Fort, (28 May, 1633). The victorious beast after putting its rival to flight, turned fiercely on Aurangzib, who firmly kept his horse from running away and struck the elephant on the forehead with his spear. A sweep of the brute's tusk hurled the horse on the ground; but Aurangzib leaped down from the saddle in time and again faced the elephant. Just then aid arrived, the animal ran away, and the prince was saved. The Emperor rewarded the heroic lad with his weight in gold.

On 13th December, 1634, Aurangzib, then 16 years of age, received his first appointment in the imperial army as a commander of ten thousand cavalry (nominal rank), and next September he was sent out to learn the art of war in the campaign against Jhujhar Singh and his son Vikramajit, the Bundela chiefs of Urchha, who were finally extirpated at the end of the year.

From 14th July, 1636 to 28th May, 1644 Aurangzib served as **viceroy of the Deccan**,—paying several visits to Northern India during the period to see the Emperor. This his first governorship of the Deccan, was marked by the conquest of Baglana and the final extinction of the Nizam-Shahi dynasty of Ahmadnagar. He was married, first to Dilras Banu, the daughter of Shah Nawaz Khan Safawi, (8th May, 1637), and at some later but unknown date to Nawab Bai, and began to have children by them, his eldest offspring being Zeb-un-nisa. the gifted poetess, (born 15th February, 1638).

In May, 1644 the prince gave up his duties and took to a life of retirement, as a protest against Dara Shukoh's jealous interference with his work and Shah Jahan's partiality to his eldest son. At this the Emperor was highly displeased, and at once deprived him of his governorship, estates, and allowances. For some months the prince lived at Agra in disgrace. But on 25th November, when Jahanara, the eldest and best beloved daughter of Shah Jahan, recovered from a terrible burn, her joyful father could refuse her nothing, and at her entreaty Aurangzib was restored to his rank. On 16th February, 1645, the viceroyalty of Gujrat was given to him ; his vigorous rule suppressed lawlessness in the province and won rewards from the Emperor.

From Gujrat Aurangzib was recalled two years later and **sent to Central Asia** to recover Balkh and Badakhshan, the cradle of the royal house of Timur. Leaving Kabul on 7th April, 1647, he reached the city of Balkh on 25th May, and battled long and arduously with the fierce enemy. The bravest Rajputs shed their blood in the Van of the Mughal army in that far off soil; immense quantities of stores, provisions and treasure were wasted; but the Indian army merely held the ground on which it encamped: the hordes of Central Asia, "more numerous than ants and locusts," and all of them born horsemen,—swarmed on all sides and could not be crushed once for all. The barren and distant conquest could have been retained only at a ruinous cost. So, a truce was patched up: Nazar Muhammad Khan, the ex-king of Balkh, was sought out with as much eagerness as Sir Lepel Griffin displayed in getting hold of the late Amir Abdur Rahman, and coaxed into taking back his throne, and the Indian army beat a hurried retreat to avoid the dreaded winter of that region. Many *krores* of Rupees of Indian revenue were thus wasted for absolutely no gain; the abandoned stores alone had cost several *lakhs*, and much property too had to be sacrificed by the rearguard for lack of transport.

During this campaign Aurangzib did an act which made his fame ring throughout the Islamic world. While the Mughal army was fighting desperately with the vast legions of Abdul Aziz Khan, king of Bukhara, the time for the evening prayer (*zuhar*) arrived. Disregarding the prohibitions of his officers, Aurangzib dismounted from his elephant, knelt down on the ground, and deliberately and peacefully went through all the ceremonies of the prayer, in full view of both the armies. Abdul Aziz on hearing of it cried out, 'To fight with such a man is to court one's own ruin' and suspended the battle.

From Balkh, Aurangzib returned to Kabul on 27th

October, 1647, and was afterwards appointed viceroy of Multan (15th March, 1648). This post he held till July, 1652, being twice in the meantime called away from his charge to **besiege Qandahar** (16th May—5th September, 1649, and 2nd May—9th July, 1652). This fort had been wrested from Shah Jahan by the Persians and these two huge and costly sieges and a third and still greater one under Dara (28th April—27th September, 1653) failed to recover it.

With his **second viceroyalty of the Deccan** (for which appointment he set out on 17th August, 1652), began the most important chapter of Aurangzib's early life. What Gaul was to Julius Cæsar as a training ground for the coming contest for empire, the Deccan was to Aurangzib. Many hundreds of his letters, preserved in the *Adab-i-Alamgiri*, give us much interesting information about his life and work during the next six years,—how he overcame his recurring financial difficulties, how he gathered a picked band of officers round himself, how ably and strenuously he ruled the country, maintaining order and securing the happiness of the people. By constant inspection and exercise he kept his army in good condition. He must have been often out on tour, as he admits in one of his letters that he was a hard rider and keen sportsman in those days. Thus the year 1658 found him beyond doubt the ablest and best equipped of the sons of Shah Jahan in the ensuing War of Succession.

At this period, too, occurred the only romance of his life, his **passion for Hira Bai**, (surnamed **Zainabadi**), whom he procured from the harem of his maternal uncle. It was a case of love at first sight and Aurangzib's infatuation for the beautiful singer knew no bound: to please her he consented to drink wine! Their union was cut short by her death in the bloom of youth, which plunged her lover in the deepest grief.

After a long intrigue he seduced from the king of Golkonda his *wazir* Mir Jumla, one of the ablest Persians who have ever served in India. At Aurangzib's recommendation Shah Jahan enrolled Mir Jumla among his officers and threw the mantle of imperial protection over him. To force the Golkonda king to give up Mir Jumla's family and property, Aurangzib made a **raid on Haidarabad** (24th January, 1656); the king fled to Golkonda where he was forced to make a humiliating peace with immense sacrifices. Mir Jumla joined Aurangzib (20th March), was summoned to Delhi and created *wazir* (7th July), and then on 18th January, 1657, returned to the Deccan to reinforce Aurangzib.

A year after this unprovoked attack on Golkonda, on the death of Muhammad Adil Shah, king of **Bijapur,** Aurangzib with his father's sanction **invaded** the latter country, (January, 1657), captured the forts of Bidar and Kaliani (29th March and 1st August respectively), and was looking forward to annexing a good deal of the territory, when the whole scene changed in the most unexpected and sudden manner.

The Emperor Shah Jahan had now reached his 66th year, and was evidently declining in health. His eldest son and intended heir-apparent, Dara Shukoh, who lived with him and conducted much of the administration, induced him to recall the additional troops sent to Aurangzib for the Bijapur war, on the very reasonable ground that the Bijapur king had thrown himself on the Emperor's mercy and offered a large indemnity and piece of territory as the price of peace. But this peremptory order to Aurangzib to come to terms with Bijapur gave him a sharp check when flushed with victory and cut short his schemes of aggression. Besides, the depletion of his army left him too weak to hold the Bijapuris to their promises, and thus the fruits of his victory were lost.

## WAR OF SUCCESSION

On 6th September, Shah Jahan was taken severely ill at Delhi. For some time his life was despaired of. Dara attended him day and night with extreme filial piety, but he also took steps to secure his own succession. He stopped the couriers on the roads and prevented his brothers from getting true news of Court affairs. But this only aggravated the evil : the wildest rumours prevailed all over the country; the Emperor was believed to be already dead ; the officers in the provinces were distracted by the prospect of an empty throne ; lawless men in all parts raised their heads without fear of punishment. Two of the princes, Murad and Shuja, openly crowned themselves in their governments, Gujrat and Bengal respectively. Aurangzib after a short period of gnawing anxiety and depressing uncertainty, decided to play a subtler game. He denounced Dara as an apostate from Islam, proclaimed his own design to be merely to free the old Emperor from Dara's domination and to purge the State from non-Islamic influences, and lastly he made an alliance with Murad Bakhsh swearing on the Quran to give him all the Mughal territory from the Panjab westwards.

Meanwhile Dara had despached two armies, one under his son Sulaiman Shukoh and Mirza Rajah Jai Singh against Shuja who was advancing from Bengal, and the other under Maharajah Jaswant Singh and Qasim Khan against Aurangzib and Murad. The first army surprised and routed Shuja at Bahadurpur, opposite Benares, (14 February, 1658), and pursued him to Mungir. But Aurangzib and Murad effected a junction outside Dipalpur and crushed Jaswant's army after a long and terribly contested **battle at Dharmat**, 14 miles south of Ujjain (15th April). Dara sent off urgent orders recalling his son from Bihar. But his division of his forces had been a fatal mistake: Sulaiman returned from far off Bihar too late to help his father or even to save himself. Aurangzib had the immense advantage of crushing his enemies piecemeal, while his own armed strength was doubled by the league with Murad.

From Ujjain the victorious brothers pushed on to the capital. **At Samugarh**, 10 miles east of Agra, **Dara** who had issued from the city with a second army, attacked them on a frightfully hot day (29th May), was signally **defeated**, and fled from Agra towards Delhi and the Panjab. Aurangzib now marched on Agra, compelled his old father to surrender the fort by stopping the supply of drinking water from the Jamuna, and kept Shah Jahan strictly confined in the harem for the remainder of his life. Then, at Mathura he treacherously **made Murad prisoner** at a banquet (25th June), and advancing to Delhi crowned himself Emperor (21st July, 1658). Dara was chased through the Panjab and Sindh to Tatta, whence he fled to Gujrat over the Rann of Cutch, undergoing terrible hardships on the way. A second army which he raised was destroyed near Ajmir (14th March, 1659), and he was hunted by Aurangzib's generals from place to place, till he reached Dadar, at the Indian mouth of the Bolan Pass, whose chief betrayed him to Aurangzib. The captive **Dara** was brought to Delhi, paraded with insult through the bazar, and **murdered** by some slaves of Aurangzib, (30th August, 1659), who had got the Mullas to issue a sentence that according to Islamic Law Dara deserved an apostate's death. **Murad Bakhsh** was **beheaded** in Gwalior prison as a judicial punishment, on the accusation of a man whose father he had slain in Gujrat, (4th December, 1661). Dara's eldest son, Sulaiman Shukoh, was secretly done to death in the same State-prison (May, 1662.)

Meantime **Shuja** had gathered together a new army and advanced beyond Allahabad to make a second attempt for the throne. But he was signally **defeated at Khajwa** (5th January 1659), and driven back to Bengal, whence after a two years' struggle on land and river he was forced to flee miserably to **Arracan** for refuge (12th May, 1660). Here he was **massacred** with his whole family for a plot against the Burmese king on whose hospitality he was living.

Thus all his rivals being removed from his path, Aurangzib became the undisputed sovereign of India.

## AURANGZIB'S REIGN IN NORTHERN INDIA

The new monarch now enjoyed a long period of comparative peace: he received grand embassies from Persia (22nd May, 1661), Bukhara (19th November, 1661), Mecca, Abyssinia (1665), and Arabia, sent to congratulate him on his accession; and the envoys were treated to a sight of the lavish splendour of the Mughal Court,—a splendour which dazzled the eyes of Bernier, Tavernier and other European travellers of the time. He had a sharp attack of illness (12th May—24th June, 1662), which threatened to shake his newly established throne; but he recovered and paid a visit to Kashmir (1st May—29th September, 1663).

Though peace reigned in the heart of the empire, there was **war on the frontiers** : ambitious and enterprising officers tried to extend their master's dominion; Daud Khan, the governor of Bihar, conquered Palamau (April—December, 1661). Mir Jumla, the governor of Bengal, overran Kuch Bihar and Assam, capturing their capitals on 19th December, 1661 and 17th March, 1662; but famine and pestilence destroyed his army, and he sank down under disease before reaching Dacca on return (31st March, 1663). Shaista Khan, the next governor of Bengal, wrested Chatgaon (Chittagong) from the Portuguese and Burmese pirates (26th January, 1666), and also captured the island of Sondip in the Bay of Bengal. An expedition from Kashmir forced the ruler of Greater Tibet to be a feudatory of the Emperor and to "submit to Islam" (November, 1665). To crown all, the able and astute general Jai Singh tamed Shivaji, the daring and hitherto invincible Maratha chief, annexed two-thirds of his forts, (Treaty of Purandhar, 11th June 1665), and induced him to do homage to the Emperor by a visit to Agra (12th May, 1666). Aurangzib's lack of statesmanship in dealing with Shivaji and the latter's romantic escape from prison (19th August) are a familiar tale all over India. True, the Mughal arms did not gain any conspicuous success in Jai Singh's invasion of Bijapur (first half of 1666), but these expeditions were of the nature of raids for extortion, and not deliberate schemes of conquest.

A more formidable but distant trouble was the revolt of the Yusufzai clan and their allies on the Afghan frontier, (begun in 1667). The war against these sturdy hillmen dragged on for many years; successive Mughal generals tried their hands and buried their military reputation there, and at last peace was purchased only by paying a large annual subsidy from the Indian revenue to these "keepers of Khaibar gate."

A state of war also continued against the Bijapur king and Shivaji for many years; but the Mughal generals were bribed by the former to carry on the contest languidly, and the latter was more than able to hold his own. These operations present us with nothing worthy of note. The Muhammadan kings of the Deccan, in fear of the Mughals, courted the alliance of Shivaji, who rapidly grew in wealth, territory, armed strength, and prestige, and had made himself the foremost power in the Deccan when death cut his activity short at the age of 52, (5th April, 1680).

Meantime Aurangzib had begun to give free play to his **religious bigotry**. In April, 1669 he ordered the provincial governors to "**destroy** all the **temples** and schools of the infidels and to utterly put down their teachings and religious practices." The wandering Hindu saint Uddhav Bairagi was confined in the police lock-up. The Vishwanath temple at Benares was pulled down in August 1669. The grandest shrine of Mathura, Kesav Rai's temple, built at a cost of 33 lakhs of Rupees by the Bundela Rajah Birsingh Dev, was razed to the ground in January, 1670, and a mosque built on its site. "The idols of this temple were brought to Agra and buried under the steps of Jahanara's mosque that they might be constantly trodden on" by the Muslims going in to pray. About this time the temple of Somnath on the south coast of the Kathiawar peninsula was demolished, and the offering of worship there ordered to be stopped. The smaller religious buildings that suffered havoc were beyond count. The Rajput War of 1679-80 was accompanied by the destruction of 240 temples in Mewar alone, including the famous one of Someshwar and three grand ones at Udaipur. In the loyal State of Jaipur 67 temples were demolished. On 2nd April, 1679, the **jazia** or poll-tax on non-Muslims was **revived**. The poor people who appealed to the Emperor and blocked a road abjectly crying for its remission, were trampled down by elephants at his order and dispersed. By another ordinance (March, 1695), "all Hindus except Rajputs were forbidden to carry arms or ride elephants, *palkis*, or Arab and Persian horses." "With one stroke of his pen he dismissed all the Hindu clerks from office." Custom duties were abolished on the Muslims and doubled on the Hindus.

The discontent provoked by such measures was an ominous sign of what their ultimate political consequence would be, though Aurangzib was too blind and obstinate to think of the future. A rebellion broke out among the peasantry in the Mathura and Agra districts, especially under Gokla Jat (1669), and the Satnamis or Mundias rose near Narnol (May, 1672), and it taxed the imperial power seriously to exterminate these 5000 stubborn peasants fighting for church and home. The Sikh Guru Tegh Bahadur was tortured in prison till he courted death as a release (1675), but his followers thereafter gave no rest to the Panjab officers.

At last Aurangzib threw off all disguise and openly **attacked the Rajputs.** Maharajah Jaswant Singh of Jodhpur died in the Emperor's service at Jamrud (10th December, 1678). Immediately Aurangzib sent out officers to take possession of his kingdom and himself marched to Ajmir to overawe opposition. Two wives of the Maharajah delivered two sons after reaching Lahor in the following February. Aurangzib sold the Jodhpur throne (May, 1679) for 36 lakhs of Rupees to a worthless grand-nephew of Jaswant and ordered the late Maharajah's widows and new-born babes to be seized and detained in his Court till the latter should come of age. But thanks to the devotion of their Rathor guards, most of whom died like heroes, and the sagacity and loyalty of Durgadas, (one of the noblest characters in Rajput history), Ajit Singh, the surviving infant of Jaswant and the future hope of the Rathor clan, was safely conveyed to Marwar (23rd July, 1679). But Aurangzib was up to any trick: he proclaimed Ajit Singh to be a counterfeit prince, and for many years cherished a beggar boy in his Court under the significant name of Muhammadi Raj, as the true son of Jaswant! All Rajputana (except ever-loyal Jaipur) burst into flame at this outrage on the head of the Rathor clan. The Maharana, Raj Singh, chivalrously took up the defence of the orphan's rights. The war dragged on with varying fortune; the country was devastated wherever the Mughals could penetrate; the Maharana took refuge in his mountain fastnesses. At last **Prince Akbar**, the fourth son of Aurangzib, **rebelled** (January, 1681), joined the Rajputs, and assumed the royal title. For a few days Aurangzib was in a most critical position, but his wonderful cunning saved him: by a false letter he sowed distrust of Akbar in the minds of the Rajputs, the prince's army melted away, and he fled, leaving all his family and property behind and reaching the Maratha Court after a perilous journey under the guidance of the faithful Durgadas (May, 1681). The Emperor patched up a peace with the Maharana (June, 1681), both sides making concessions. But henceforth the Rajputs ceased to be supporters of the Mughal throne; we no longer read of large Rajput contingents fighting under the imperial banner; he had to depend more on the Bundelas. The Rathors continued the war till the close of Aurangzib's life. Here ends the first and stable half of Aurangzib's reign—the period passed in Northern India.

## AURANGZIB'S REIGN IN THE DECCAN

We next enter on a scene of unceasing but fruitless exertion for 26 years, the war with the "slim" Marathas, which ruined the Emperor's health, the *morale* of his army, and the finances of the State,—a war of which all saw the futility and all were heartily tired, all save Aurangzib, who pursued one policy with increasing obstinacy, till at last the old man of 90 sank into the grave amidst despair darkness, and chaos ready to overwhelm his family and empire.

Shivaji's eldest son Shambhu was a more daring raider than his father and deterred by no fear of consequences. With Akbar as his pensioner, what might he not do against the Mughal crown ? Moreover, all of Aurangzib's generals and even his sons sent against the kingdoms of the Deccan had failed of conquest, and were rightly suspected of corruption. So there was nothing left for Aurangzib but to conduct the war in person. With this object he left Ajmir for the Deccan (8th September, 1681), never again to return to Northern India alive or dead. The capital Aurangabad was reached on 22nd March, 1682. Thence, on 13th November, 1683, he arrived at Ahmadnagar, a town to which he was destined to return 23 years afterwards only to die. Two of his sons and some nobles were despatched against the Bijapuris and the Marathas, but they effected nothing decisive, though a large number of Shambhu's forts were captured. A large force which penetrated through the Ram-ghat pass into Southern Konkan under Prince Muazzam, returned with failure and heavy loss (September, 1683—May, 1684).

Fierce as was Aurangzib's hatred of the Hindus (the vast majority of his subjects), it was equalled by his **aversion for the Shias**,—who supplied him with some of his best generals and all his ablest civil officers. To him the Shia was a heretic (*rafizi*); in one of his letters he quotes with admiration the story of a Sunni who escaped to Turkey after murdering a Shia at Isfahan, and draws from it the moral, "Whoever acts for truth and speaks up for truth, is befriended by the True God!" In another letter he tells us how he liked the naming of a dagger as the 'Shia-slayer' (*Rafizi kush*), and ordered some more of the same name to be made for him. In his correspondence he never mentions the Shias without an abusive epithet: 'corpse-eating demons' (*ghul-i-bayabani*), 'misbelievers' (*batil mazhaban*) are among his favourite phrases. Indeed, even the highest Shia officers had such a bad time of it in his Court that they often played the hypocrite to please him! Aurangzib threw the cloak of Sunni orthodoxy over his aggressive conquest of Bijapur and Golkonda, of which the rulers were Shias. The Chief Qazi Shaikh-ul-Islam (one of the purest characters of the age) tried to dissuade the Emperor from these "wars between Muslims" as opposed to Islam. But Aurangzib grew displeased at the opposition ; the honest and manly Qazi resigned his post, left the Court, and for the rest of his life rejected the Emperor's repeated solicitations to resume his high office.

On 1st April, 1685, the **siege of Bijapur** was begun by Prince Azam and Khan-i-Jahan Bahadur. The Emperor advanced to Sholapur (24th May) to be near the seat of war. A terrible famine desolated the besiegers; but reinforcements soon arrived with provisions, though scarcity of a kind continued in a chronic state in the Mughal camp. The relieving armies of Berads and Marathas were beaten back and the siege pressed on. The garrison fought with the heroism of despair. Aurangzib himself arrived in the environs of the city to superintend the siege operations (3rd July, 1686). At last on 12th September, Sikandar, the last of the Adil-Shahi kings, surrendered, and his kingdom was annexed.

Meantime another force had been sent under Prince Muazzam or Shah Alam (28th June, 1685) against

Golkonda to prevent aid from coming from that quarter to Bijapur. It captured the rich city of Haidarabad, making an immense loot (October). The king, Abul Hasan, a worthless voluptuary and the exact counterpart of Wajid Ali of Oudh, helplessly **shut** himself **up** in the **Fort of Golkonda.** But his chiefs were seduced by the Mughals; there was discontent among his Muhammadan officers at the power of his Brahman minister Madanna Pant. Aurangzib himself arrived near Golkonda on 28th January, 1687, and began its siege. The besiegers had a hard time of it before that impregnable fort: a terrible famine raged in Haidarabad, but the rains and swollen rivers rendered the transport of grain impossible, and the most ghastly scenes were acted by the sufferers. At an immense cost the Mughals filled the moat up and also erected a huge barrier wall of wood and clay completely surrounding the fort and preventing ingress and egress. But mining and assault failed, and it was only the treachery of a Golkonda officer that opened the gate of the fort to the Mughals at midnight (21st September, 1687). The king was dragged out and sent to share the captivity of his brother of Bijapur. His kingdom was annexed. Two years later, **Shambhuji,** the brave but dissolute Maratha king, was surprised by an energetic Deccani officer (Muqarrab Khan), ignominiously paraded through the imperial camp like a wild beast, and **executed** with prolonged and inhuman tortures (11th March, 1689). His capital Raigarh was captured (19th October) and his entire family, "mothers, wives, daughters, and sons" made prisoner by the Mughals. His eldest son, Shahu, was brought up at the imperial Court in gilded fetters.

All seemed to have been gained by Aurangzib now, but in reality all was lost. It was **the beginning of his end.** The saddest and most hopeless chapter of his life now opened. The Mughal empire had become too large to be ruled by one man or from one centre. Aurangzib, like the boa constrictor, had swallowed more than he could digest. It was impossible for him to take possession of all the provinces of the newly annexed kingdoms and at the same time to suppress the Marathas. His enemies rose on all sides, he could defeat but not crush them for ever. As soon as his army marched away from a place, the enemy who had been hovering round occupied it again, and Aurangzib's work was undone! Lawlessness reigned in many places of Northern and Central India. The old Emperor in the far off Deccan lost control over his officers in Hindustan, and the **administration grew slack** and corrupt; chiefs and zamindars defied the local authorities and asserted themselves, filling the country with tumult. In the province of Agra in particular, there was chronic disorder. Art and learning decayed at the withdrawal of imperial patronage, —not a single grand edifice, finely written manuscript, or exquisite picture commemorates Aurangzib's reign. The endless war in the Deccan exhausted his treasury; the Government turned bankrupt; the soldiers, starving from arrears of pay, mutinied; and during the closing years of his reign the revenue of Bengal, regularly sent by the faithful and able diwan Murshid Quli Khan, was the sole support of the Emperor's household and army, and its arrival was eagerly looked forward to, Napoleon I. used to say, "It was the Spanish ulcer which ruined me." The Deccan ulcer ruined Aurangzib.

To resume the narrative, imperial officers were despatched to all sides to take over the forts and provinces of the two newly annexed kingdoms from their local officers, many of whom had set up for themselves. The Berads, a wild Kanarese tribe, whom Col. Meadows Taylor has described in his fascinating *Story of My Life*, were the first to be attacked. Their country, situated between Bijapur and Golkonda, was overrun, their capital Sagar captured (28th Nov., 1687), and their chief Pid Naik, a strongly built uncouth black savage, brought to the Court. But the brave and hardy clansmen rose under other leaders and the Mughals had to send two more expeditions against them.

A desolating epidemic of **bubonic plague** broke out in Bijapur (early in November, 1688), sparing neither prince nor peasant. The imperial household paid toll to Death in the persons of Aurangabadi Mahal (a wife of the Emperor), Fazil Khan the *Sadr*, and the bogus son of Jaswant Singh. Of humbler victims the number is said to have reached a *lakh*.

After Shambhu's capture, his younger brother Rajaram made a hair-breadth escape to the fort of Jinji, (Gingee in the S. Arcot district of Madras), which was besieged by the Mughal general Zulfiqar Khan Nusrat Jang and Prince Kam Bakhsh (Septemper, 1690), and fell on 7th January, 1698. Two years afterwards Rajaram, the last king of the Marathas, died. But the **Maratha** captains, each acting on his own account, incessantly raided the Mughal territory and did the greatest possible injury by their **guerilla warfare**. The two ablest, most successful, and most dreaded leaders of this class were Dhana Singh Jadav and Santa Ghorpare (and latterly Nima Sindhia), who dealt heavy blows at some important Mughal detachments. They seemed to be ubiquitous and elusive like the wind. The movable columns frequently sent from the imperial head-quarters to "chastise the robbers," only marched and counter-marched, without being able to crush the enemy. When the Mughal force had gone back the scattered Marathas, like water parted by the oar, closed again and resumed their attack, as if nothing had happened to them.

## THE LAST PHASE

After moving about almost every year between Bijapur in the south and the Manjira river in the north, Aurangzib (21st May, 1695) finally made Brahmapuri, on the Bhima river east of Pandharpur, his Base **Camp**, and named it **Islampuri**. Here a city sprang up from his encampment, and it was walled round in time. Here his family was lodged when he went forth on campaigns.

On 19th October, 1699, after a four years' stay at Islampuri, Aurangzib, now aged 81 years, set out to **besiege the Maratha forts in person**. The rest of his life is a repetition of the same sickening tale: a hill fort captured by him after a great loss of time men and money, the fort recovered by the Marathas from the weak Mughal garrison after a few months, and the siege begun again by the Emperor after a year or two ! The soldiers and camp-followers suffered unspeakable hardships in marching over flooded rivers, muddy roads and broken hilly tracks; porters disappeared, transport beasts died of hunger and overwork, scarcity of grain was ever present in the camp. His officers all wearied of this labour of Sisyphus ; but Aurangzib would burst into wrath at any suggestion of return to Hindustan and taunt the unlucky counsellor with cowardice and love of ease ! The mutual jealousies of his generals, Nusrat Jang and Firuz Jang, Shujaet Khan and Muhammad Murad Khan, Tarbiyat Khan and Fathullah Khan, spoiled his affairs as thoroughly as the French cause in the Peninsular War was ruined by the jealousies of Napoleon's marshals. Therefore, the Emperor must conduct every operation in person or nothing would be done!

A bare record of his sieges will suffice here :

BASANTGARH (siege, 22nd—25th Nov., 1699).

SATARA (siege, 8th Dec., 1699—21 April, 1700).

PARLIGARH near Satara (siege, 30th April—9th June).

*Halt at Khawaspur for the rainy season* of 1700, (30th Aug.—16 Dec.)

PANHALA (siege, 9th March—28th May, 1701) also Pavangarh captured.

*Halt at Khatau for the rainy season* of 1701, (29th May—7th Nov.)

Capture of Wardhangarh (6th June, 1701), Nandgir, Chandan and Wandan (6th Oct.) by Fathullah Khan.

KHELNA (siege, 26th Dec., 1701—4th June, 1702).

*The rainy season* of 1702 spent in a most painful march (10th June—13 Nov.) from Khelna to Bahadurgarh with a month's halt at Vadgaon in August.

KONDANA (siege, 27th December, 1702—8th April, 1703).

*Halt at Puna for the rainy season* of 1703, (1st May—10th November).

RAJGARH (siege, 2nd Dec. 1703—16th Feby. 1704).

TORNA (siege, 23rd February—10th March).

*Halt at Khed for the rainy season* of 1704 (17th April —21st October.)

WAGINGERA (siege, 8th February—27th April, 1705).

*Halt at Devapur*, 8 miles from Wagingera, *for the rainy season* of 1705, (*c.* 1st May—23rd October).

This was the last of his sieges, for here he got a warning of what was to come. At Devapur a severe illness attacked him, which was aggravated by his insistence on transacting business as usual. The whole camp was in despair and confusion : who would extricate them from that gloomy mountainous region if the Emperor died ? At last Aurangzib yielded to their entreaty and probably also to the warning of approaching death, and **retreated** to Bahadurpur (6th December 1705), whence he reached **Ahmadnagar** (20th January, 1706), to die a year later.

The last years of Aurangzib's life were inexpressibly sad. On its public side there was the consciousness that his long reign of half a century had been a colossal failure. "After me will come the deluge !" this morose foreboding of Louis XV. was repeated by Aurangzib almost word for word (*Az ma-st hamah fasad-i-baqi*). His domestic life, too, was loveless and dreary, and wanting in the benign peace and hopefulness which throw a halo round old age. A sense of unutterable loneliness haunted the heart of Aurangzib in his old age. One daughter, Zinat-un-nisa, already an old maid, looked after his household, and his youngest concubine, Udaipuri, bore him company. But he had at one time or other, to imprison all his five sons except one ! By his own conduct in the War of Succession he had raised a spectre which relentlessly pursued him :

what if *his* sons should treat him in his weak old age as he had treated Shah Jahan ? This fear of Nemesis ever haunted his mind, and he had no peace while his sons were with him! Lastly, there was the certainty of a deluge of blood when he would close his eyes, and his three surviving sons, each supported by a provincial army and treasury, would fight for the throne to the bitter end. In two most pathetic letters written to his sons when he felt the sure approach of death, the old Emperor speaks of the alarm and distraction of his soldiery, the passionate grief of Udaipuri, and his own bitter sense of the futility of his life, and then entreats them not to cause the slaughter of Musalmans by engaging in a civil war among themselves. A paper, said to have been found under his pillow after his death, contained a plan for the peaceful partition of the empire among his three sons. Meantime death was also busy at work within his family circle. When Gauharara, the last among Aurangzib's brothers and sisters, died, (about March, 1706), he felt that his own turn would come soon. Some of his nephews, daughters, and grandsons, too, were snatched away from him in the course of his last year. In the midst of the darkness closing around him he used to hum the pathetic verses :—

By the time you have reached your 80th or 90th year,
You must have met with many a hard blow from the hand of Time ;
And when from that point you reach the stage of a hundred,
Death will put on the form of your life.

And also,—

In a twinkle, in a minute, in a breath,
The condition of the world changes.

His last illness overtook him at Ahmadnagar, early

in February 1707; then he rallied for 5 or 6 days, sent away his two sons from his camp to their provincial governments, and went through business and daily prayers regularly. But that worn out frame of 91 years had been taxed too much. A severe fever set in, and in the morning of Friday, 20th February, 1707, he gradually sank down exhausted into the arms of death, with the Muslim confession of faith on his lips and his fingers on his rosary.

The corpse was despatched to Khuldabad, six miles from Daulatabad, and there buried in the courtyard of the tomb of the saint Shaikh Zain-ud-din, in a red sandstone sepulchre built by Aurangzib in his own lifetime. The covering slab, 9 feet by 7 feet, is only a few inches in height, and has a cavity in the middle which is filled with earth for planting green herbs in.

Aurangzib's wife, DILRAS BANU BEGAM, the daughter of Shah Nawaz Khan Safawi, died on 8th October, 1657, after bearing him Zeb-un-nisa, Azam and Akbar. A secondary wife (*mahal*) NAWAB BAI, the mother of Sultan and Muazzam, does not seem to have been a favourite, as her husband seldom sought her society after his accession. Of his three concubines (*parastar*), Hira Bai or ZAINABADI, with whom he was infatuated almost to madness, died very young; AURANGABADI, the mother of Mihr-un-nisa died of the plague in November 1688; UDAIPURI, the favourite companion of Aurangzib's old age and the mother of his pet son Kam Bakhsh, entered his harem after his accession. She is said to have been a Circassian slave-girl of Dara, gained by Aurangzib among the spoils of victory. But another account which describes her as a Kashmiri woman is more likely to be true, because the *Masir-i-Alamgiri* calls her *Bai*, a title which was applied to Hindu women only. Her descent from the royal house of Mewar is a fanciful conjecture of some modern writers.

Aurangzib's eldest son, SULTAN, chafing under the restraints of his father's officers, during the war of succession in Bengal, fled to Shuja and married his daughter, but in a few months returned to his father. The foolish youth, then only 20 years old, was kept in prison for the rest of his life. (Died 3rd December, 1676).

His second son, MUAZZAM, (also *Shah Alam*), who in 1707 succeeded him on the throne as Bahadur Shah I., incensed Aurangzib by intriguing with the besieged kings of Bijapur and Golkonda, and was placed in confinement (21st February, 1687). After his spirit had been thoroughly tamed, his captivity was relaxed little by little (in a rather amusing fashion), and at last, on 9th May, 1695, he was sent to the Panjab as governor, (afterwards getting Afghanistan also to govern).

The third prince, AZAM, stepped into the vacant place of the heir-apparent (*Shah-i-alijah*) during Muazzam's disgrace, and was made much of by his father. But he was extremely haughty, prone to anger, and incapable of self-restraint.

The fourth, AKBAR, rebelled against his father in 1681, and fled to Persia where he died an exile in November, 1704. His presence at Farah, on the Khurasan frontier, was long a menace to the peace of India.

The youngest, KAM BAKHSH, the spoilt child of his father's old age, was worthless, self-willed, and foolish.

For his misconduct during the siege of Jinji he was put under restraint, and again confined for his fatuous attachment to his foster-brother, a wretch who had tried to assassinate an excellent officer. The third and fifth brothers fell fighting in the struggle for the throne which followed Aurangzib's death, (1707 and 1709).

## AURANGZIB'S CHARACTER

So lived and so died Aurangzib, surnamed Alamgir Padishah, the last of the Great Mughals. For, in spite of his religious intolerance, narrowness of mind and lack of generosity and statesmanship, he was great in the possession of some qualities which might have gained for him the highest place in any sphere of life except the supreme one of ruling over men. He would have made a successful general, minister, theologian or school-master, and an ideal departmental head. But the critical eminence of a throne on which he was placed by a freak of Fortune, led to the failure of his life and the blighting of his fame.

Pure in his domestic relations, simple and abstemious like a hermit, he had a passion for work and a hatred of ease and pleasure which remind one of George Grenville, though with Grenville's untiring industry he had also Grenville's narrowness and obstinacy. European travellers observed with wonder the grey-headed Emperor holding open Court every day, reading every petition and writing orders across it with his own hand. Of the letters dictated by him, those that are known to exist in Europe and India, number about two thousand. (I have got copies of all of them as far as known to me). Many more must have perished.

In matters of official discipline and Court etiquette he was a martinet and enforced the strictest obedience to rules and established usages: "If I suffer a single regulation to be violated, all of them will be disregarded," was his frequent remark. But this punctilious observance of the form must have led to neglect of the spirit of institutions and laws.

His passion for doing everything himself and dictating the minutest particulars to far off governors and generals, robbed them of all self-reliance and power of initiative, and left them hesitating and helpless in the face of any unexpected emergency. His suspicious policy crushed the latent ability of his sons, so that at his death they were no better than children though turned of fifty years of age. Alike in his passion for work, distrust of the men on the spot, preference for incompetent but servile agents, and religious bigotry, he resembled his contemporary in Europe, Louis XIV.

His coolness and courage were famous throughout India: no danger however great, no emergency however unlooked for, could shake his heart or cloud the serene light of his intellect. Indeed, he regarded danger as only the legitimate risk of greatness. No amount of exertion could fatigue that thin wiry frame. The privations of a campaign or forced ride had no terror for him. Of diplomacy he was a past master, and could not be beaten in any kind of intrigue or secret manipulation. He was as much a "master of the pen" as a "master of the sword."

From the strict path of a Muslim king's duty as laid down in the Quranic Law nothing could make him deviate in the least. And he was also determined not to let *others* deviate too! No fear of material loss or influence of any favourite, no tears or supplication could induce him to act contrary to the *Shara* (Canon Law). Flatterers styled him "a living saint," (*Alamgir zinda pir*). Indeed, from a very early period of his life he had chosen "the strait gate and narrow way which leadeth unto life"; but the defects of his heart made the gate straiter and the way narrower.

He lacked that warm generosity of the heart, that chivalry to fallen foes, and that easy familiarity of address in private life, which made the great Akbar win the love and admiration of his contemporaries and of all posterity. Like the English Puritans, Aurangzib drew his inspiration from the old law of relentless punishment and vengeance and forgot that mercy is an attribute of the Supreme Judge of the Universe.

His cold intellectuality, his suspicious nature, and his fame for profound statecraft, chilled the love of all who came near him. Sons, daughters, generals, and ministers, all feared him with a secret but deep-rooted fear, which neither respect nor flattery could disguise.

Art, music, dance, and even poetry (other than "familiar quotations") were his aversion, and he spent his leisure hours in hunting for legal precedents in Arabic works on Jurisprudence.

Scrupulously following the rules of the Quran in his own private life, he considered it his duty to enforce them on everybody else; the least deviation from the strict and narrow path of Islamic orthodoxy in any part of his dominions, would (he feared) endanger his own soul. His spirit was therefore the narrow and selfish spirit of the lonely recluse, who seeks his individual salvation, oblivious of the outside world. A man possessed with such ideas may have made a good *faqir*,—though Aurangzib lacked the *faqir's* noblest quality, charity;—but he was the worst ruler imaginable of an empire composed of many creeds and races, of diverse interests and ways of life and thought.

"The nature of man is intricate; the objects of society are of the greatest possible complexity: and therefore no simple disposition or direction of power can be suitable either to man's nature, or to the quality of his affairs......Political reason is a computing principle; adding, subtracting, multiplying, and dividing true moral denominations......The true lawgiver ought to have an heart full of sensibility. He ought to love and respect his kind, and to fear himself. Political arrangement is to be only wrought by social means. There mind must conspire with mind." (*Burke*).

Aurangzib utterly lacked sympathy, imagination, breadth of vision, elasticity in the choice of means, and that warmth of the heart which atones for a hundred faults of the head. These limitations of his character completely undermined the Mughal empire, so that on his death it suddenly fell in a single downward plunge. Its inner life was gone, and the outward form could not deceive the world long. Time relentlessly sweeps away whatever is inefficient, unnecessary, or false to Nature.

# ANECDOTES OF AURANGZIB

## INTRODUCTION

In 1903, Mr. William Irvine, I.C.S. (retired), the historian of the Later Mughals, in his usual spirit of help to younger men engaged in research, lent me a work (numbered by him 252) from his private collection of Persian MSS. which was not known to exist in any other library of Europe or India and which no historian had yet used. It was the *Ahkam-i-Alamgiri*, attributed to the pen of Hamid-ud-din Khan (surnamed Nimchah-i-Alamgiri), whose life is given in the *Masir-ul-umara*, i. 605—611. But of this authorship there is no proof, and none of the three MSS. bears his name. Subsequently Mr. Irvine sent me another and earlier MS. of the *Ahkam*, (No 340 of his library), of which No. 252 is only a copy. I made a transcript of the book, carefully collating the two MSS. In 1905, I discovered another fragment of this work bound up with some letters of Aurangzib, with the leaves put together in disorder, in the India Office Library Persian MS. 3388. In October 1907, I found at Rampur (Rohilkhand) a fourth copy, identical with Mr. Irvine's in extent and arrangement of matter, but more correct and supplying useful variants. The owner, Nawab Abdus Salam Khan Bahadur, retired Sub-Judge, Oudh, very kindly permitted me to take a copy of it. This gentleman possesses another MS. of the work, which he has named *Sharah-i-dastkhat-i-Alamgiri*. It is incomplete and covers a portion of the India Office MS. (the arrangement, however, being different). There is only one new anecdote in it, which I here print as § 51.

On the basis of these four MSS. (*viz.*, Irvine No. 252 collated with 340, I. O. L. No. 3388, and the longer Rampur copy), I have edited the Persian text and made the following English translation of it. The division of the book and the arrangement of the anecdotes are my own. The passages printed in thick type are in Arabic in the original, and have been translated with the kind help of Prof. Abdul Hai of Patna College.

*Abbreviations.*

*Nuskha A* = Irvine MS. No. 340.

Ir. MS. = Irvine MS. No. 252, *(Nuskha B.)*

MS. N. = India Office MS. No. 3388 *(Nuskha N.)*

MS. R = Rampur (Abdus Salam Khan's) first MS. of the *Ahkam*, *(Nuskha R.)*

*A.N.* = *Alamgirnamah.*

*Pad.* = *Padishahnamah* by Abdul Hamid Lahori.

*M. U.* = *Masir-ul-umara*
*M.A.* = *Masir-i-Alamgiri*
Khafi Khan = *Muntakhab-ul-labab*
} The last five works are of the Bibliotheca Indica edition.

My Persian text mainly follows Irvine MS. 252.

# ANECDOTES OF AURANGZIB

(*Translated from the Persian*)

SECTION I.

## ABOUT AURANGZIB HIMSELF

### § 1. Young Aurangzib fights with an elephant.

WHEN the Emperor Shah Jahan was staying at Lahor, he often engaged in [witnessing] elephant-combats in the garden of Shalamar. Once the governor of Bengal sent him 40 highly praised fighting elephants. The Emperor sat at the balcony, while the four princes (his sons) witnessed the sport from horseback. One elephant fleeing from its opponent came towards the princes. Three of the Emperor's sons fled to the right and left. Only Muhammad Aurangzib, who was fourteen years old, stood firmly without moving at all. The runaway elephant passed by him. The pursuing prince charged it with the spear he held in his hand. A blow from the elephant's trunk hurled the horse down to the ground. Aurangzib leaped up and seizing the spear again turned to the elephant in order to throw it at its head. At this juncture the servants came up, and the Emperor in great agitation descended from the balcony. Aurangzib slowly proceeded towards his Majesty. Itimad Khan, the *nazir*, who had come near,—on the strength of his being an old servant, he having come over to the Emperor's service from the house of the prince's maternal grandfather Asaf Khan,—

cried out in a loud tone, "You are coming away slowly, while the Emperor is in an awful state [of alarm]." The prince replied in a low tone, "If the elephant were here I might have walked faster. But *now* there is no reason to be agitated!" When Aurangzib reached his father, the Emperor presented one lakh of Rupees as propitiatory offerings (*nisar*) for the prince and said, "My child, thank God that it has ended well! If (God forbid it!) the matter had taken a different turn, what a dishonour would it have been!" Aurangzib salamed and replied, "If it had ended differently there would have been no dishonour in it. The shame lay in what my brothers did. [*Verse*]

Death drops the screen even over emperors,
What dishonour is there in it?"

*Text.*—Ir. MS. 15*a* & *b*, MS. N. 25*b*—26*b*.

*Notes.*—The true account of the incident is thus given in the *Padishahnamah* of Abdul Hamid, i. A. 489-492:—Shah Jahan was witnessing an elephant combat from the balcony of Agra Fort (28th May, 1633). His three elder sons were on horseback on the ground. Two elephants named Sudhakar (tusked) and Suratsundar (tuskless) were ordered to fight. Sudhakar, on seeing its rival running away, charged Aurangzib, who kept his horse from turning back, and wounded the elephant on the forehead with his spear. The fireworks (rockets, *charkhis*, &c.) discharged by the servants had no effect on the elephant, which felled Aurangzib's horse with its *tusk* (not trunk). Aurangzib jumped down from the saddle in time. Shuja, forcing his way through the crowd and smoke, struck the brute with his spear, but his horse reared and threw him down. Jai Singh's horse shied. Meantime Suratsundar returned to the attack, and Sudhakar ran away from the princes. Aurangzib was just 14 years of age at the time. The Emperor presented him with

5,000 gold coins, the elephant Sudhakar, and other gifts of the total value of two *lakhs* of Rupees.

Itimad Khan was an eunuch presented to Shah Jahan by his father-in-law, Yamin-ud-daula Asaf Khan.

## § 2. Aurangzib's early jealousy of Dara.

A mansion had been [newly] built at Agra for Dara Shukoh. He invited to it Shah Jahan and his three other sons. As it was the summer season, an underground room had been constructed close to the river, and mirrors from Aleppo, longer than the human stature, had been hung on the side towards the river. Dara conducted Shah Jahan and his brothers to see how the room looked. Muhammad Aurangzib sat down close to the door leading in and out of the room. Dara seeing it winked at the Emperor, as if to say 'See where he is sitting.' His Majesty said, "My child, though I know you to be learned and hermit-like, yet it is also needful to maintain one's rank. [There is a popular saying],—'If you do not maintain your rank, you are an atheist.' What necessity is there for you to sit down in the path by which people pass, and in a position below your younger brother?" Aurangzib replied, "I shall afterwards tell you the reason of my sitting down here." After a short time he rose on the plea of performing his midday prayer (*zuhar*) in congregation, and went back from the place to his own house without taking the Emperor's permission. When the Emperor heard of it he forbade him the Court, so that the prince was debarred from the audience for seven months. After the seven months, the Emperor told the Begam Sahib [Jahanara, the Crown Princess], "Go to

3

his house and learn for me the reason of his coming back on that day without my leave and of his sitting down on a low level." When the Begam Sahib went and asked him, he replied, "On the day when Dara Shukoh had invited us, if that brother intentionally so acted that, after making his father and three brothers sit down in that underground room with one door, he repeatedly came in and went out for the necessary supervision of the entertainment, [I feared that] he might shut the door, and then all would be over [with us]. If he acted thus through carelessness, it repeatedly struck me that I should do the work (of guarding the door) while he was inside the room. But His Majesty out of a sense of dignity forbade my action. So I came out after begging God's pardon." Immediately on hearing this the Emperor summoned the prince and conferred favours on him. The prince told Sadullah Khan [the prime-minister], "Send me away from the Court by any means that you can, as I have lost my sleep and peace of mind." So His Majesty sent him from Lahor to act as governor of the Deccan.

*Text.*—Ir. MS. 15*b*—16*a*; MS. N. 24*a*—25*b*.

*Notes.*—*Lahor* in the last sentence must be a mistake for *Multan*. Aurangzib was never subahdar of Lahor (the Panjab), but on 14th July, 1652 he was appointed subahdar of the Deccan on transfer from Multan.

On 1st December, 1645 Dara was given two *lakhs* of Rupees for his new house on the Jamuna *at Delhi* (Abdul Hamid's *Padishahnamah*, ii. 474). This house was visited by Shah Jahan on 14th March, 1643 (*Ibid.* 333). Dara's house on the bank of the Jamuna at *Agra* was inhabited by the Emperor from 20th July to 8th August, 1644 (*Ibid.* 380, 386). Aurangzib was in disgrace at Agra from 28 May to 25th November, 1644

*(Ibid.* 376, 398) and was afterwards (16th February, 1645) sent as subahdar to Gujrat (411). The Emperor again visited Dara's house at Agra on 2nd January, 1645 (403).

## § 3. Young Aurangzib's courtesy to Nobles.

Dara Shukoh behaved towards some of the nobles with enmity and towards some others with arrogance,—such as Ali Mardan Khan, Sadullah Khan, and Sayyid Miran of Barha, who were commanders of five thousand each and intimate courtiers of Shah Jahan. But Aurangzib had a special friendship with every one of them ; so that in his letters he used to address Ali Mardan Khan, (on whom Shah Jahan had bestowed the title of 'Faithful Friend'), with the friendly epithet of 'Man of good deeds' ; to address Sadullah Khan (who had the titles of 'Staff of old age' and 'Minister full of plans', and of whom Aurangzib, by reason of his having read with him, regarded himself as a pupil), as 'Minister full of plans' and 'the Head of humble pupils' ; and Sayyid Miran of Barha, whom the Emperor had entitled 'the Sayyid of Sayyids', as 'The essence of the descendants of His Holiness the Sayyid of the Universe (*i.e.*, Muhammad)'. Every one of these three nobles, and others besides them such as Afzal Khan Mulla Ala-ul-mulk (who from the rank of *khan-i-saman* afterwards attained to the post of *wazir*), in their extreme love for Aurangzib did every service required by friendship in guarding his interests in his absence. His Majesty Shah Jahan was deeply grieved at heart. On seeing the signs of [future] misfortune on the forehead of *Shah-i-buland-iqbal* (Dara Shukoh) and the marks of rise in the fortune of Aurangzib, he advised Dara against his bad acts and words. But when he found that Dara Shukoh did not profit by the good counsel, as has been well said, (*Verse*)

> If the blanket of a man's Fate has been woven black,
> Even the waters of the Zimzim and Kausar* cannot wash it white,

he wished that Muhammad Aurangzib should change his behaviour to the nobles so that they might give up protecting him in his absence.

On a royal letter he wrote in his own hand to Aurangzib, "My child! it is proper for kings and their sons to have a lofty spirit and to display elevation of mind. I have heard that in dealing with every one of my officers you show the greatest humility on your part. If you do so with a view to the future, [know that] all things depend on predestination, and that nothing but contempt will be gained by this meekness of spirit." Aurangzib replied, "What your Majesty has, out of favour and kindness, written with your gracious pen concerning this humble slave, has come down **like a revelation from the heavens.** Hail, true saint and spiritual guide! **'Thou givest honour to whomsoever Thou wishest and disgrace to whom Thou desirest,'** [this text proves that honour and lowliness] are solely dependent on the predestination of the Master of Slaves and Creator of Earth and Cities. I am acting according to the true Tradition narrated by Anas the son of Malik, **'whosoever humbles himself, God bestows honour on him.'** I consider wounding the hearts [of others] as the worst of sins and the most shameful of vices. I am not

---

* Ẓimzim is a sacred well at Mecca and Kausar is a spring of heaven.

contradicting what has been written in your gracious letter, but I know for certain that it was written agreeably to [the verse] '**The temptations of the Devil, who creates suspicion in the hearts of men; and he is one of the genii and men.**' (*Verse*)

I cannot say anything except excuses for my sins.
Pardon the sins of me, a wretch with a blackened face
and dark record!"

*Text.*—Ir. MS. 22*b*—23*b*.

*Notes.*—Mulla Ala-ul-mulk Tuni was created Fazil Khan (not *Afzal*) and *khan-i-saman* by Shah Jahan (*M. U.* iii. 524—530). Aurangzib appointed him *diwan*, *i. e. wazir*, on 7th June, 1663, but he died on the 23rd. (*M. A.* 46). Anas ibn Malik (d. 93 A. H.) was the last of the Companions of Muhammad and the founder of the Maliki sect.

## § 4. Shah Jahan's estimate of his sons.

The Emperor Shah Jahan used to say, "At times I fear that my eldest son [Dara Shukoh] has become the enemy of good men; Murad Bakhsh has set his heart on drinking; Muhammad Shuja has no good trait except contentment (*i. e.*, easy good nature). But the resolution and intelligence of Aurangzib prove that he [alone] can shoulder this difficult task (*viz.*, ruling India). But there is great sickness and infirmity in his physical frame. (*Verse*)

Then, whom will he wish for as a friend
and to whom will his heart incline?"

*Text.*—Ir. MS. 14*a*. Not in MS. N. This anecdote occurs in many other collections and is No. 5 in the lithographed *Ruqaat-i-Alamgiri*.

## § 5. Love-affair with Zainabadi.

The affair of Zainabadi happened in this manner:

At the time when Aurangzib was made governor of the Deccan and was going to Aurangabad [his head-quarters], on arriving at Burhanpur, the governor of which was Saif Khan, (who had married the prince's maternal aunt, *viz.* Saliha Banu, the daughter of Asaf Khan), he went to visit her, and she too had invited him. As it was the house of his aunt, not much care was taken to remove the women of the harem out of his view, and the prince entered the house without announcing himself. Zainabadi, whose original name was Hira Bai, was standing under a tree, holding a branch with her right hand and singing in a low tone. Immediately on seeing her, the prince unable to control himself, sat down there, and then fell down at full length on the ground in a swoon. The news was carried to his aunt. Running barefooted [to the place] she clasped him to her breast and began to wail and lament. After 3 or 4 *gharis* the prince regained consciousness. However much she inquired about his condition, asking, 'What malady is it ? Did you ever have any attack of it before?' the prince gave no reply at all but remained silent. The joy of the entertainment and hospitality was destroyed, and the affair turned into mourning and grief. It was midnight when the prince recovered his speech, and said, "If I mention my disease, can you apply the remedy ?" When his aunt heard these words, she in extreme gladness gave away propitiatory alms (*tasadduq*), made sacrifices (*qurban*), and said, "What do you talk of remedy ? I shall offer my life itself [to cure you]." Then the prince revealed the whole matter to her. On hearing it, she (almost) lost her consciousness and became tongue-tied, not knowing what to answer. At last the prince said, "You have uselessly shown all this tenderness in inquiring after my health. When you are not giving a reply to my words, how can you cure me ?" The aunt replied, "May I be your sacrifice ! You know this wretch, (*viz.*, Saif Khan); he is a bloodthirsty man, and does not care in the least for the Emperor Shah Jahan or yourself. On merely hearing of your request (for Hira Bai) he will first murder her and then me. Telling him (about your passion) will do no other good than this that I shall have to sacrifice my life. But why should the life of that poor innocent girl be destroyed for no offence ?" The prince replied, "Indeed, you have spoken the truth. I shall try some other device."

After sunrise he came back to his own house, and did not eat anything at all. Summoning Murshid Quli Khan, who was the prince's subordinate and diwan of the Deccan, he discussed the case in detail with him, as he was his trusted confidant of secrets. The Khan said, "Let me first despatch him (*i. e.*, murder Saif Khan), and if afterwards anybody slays me, there will be no harm, as in exchange of my blood-price the work of my saint and spiritual guide (*i. e.*, the prince) will be achieved." The prince replied, "Indeed, I know that you are so ready to scrifice your life for me. But my heart does not consent to making my aunt a widow. Besides, according to the Quranic Law, one cannot undertake a manifest murder with a knowledge of religious law. You should speak [to Saif Khan], relying on God [for success]." Murshid Quli Khan set off without any grumbling and told everything to Saif

Khan, who replied, "Convey my *salam* to the prince. I shall give the answer of this to his maternal aunt." That very moment he went to the women's apartments and told [his wife], "What harm is there in it? I have no need for [Aurangzib's] Begam, the daughter of Shah Nawaz Khan. Let him send me Chattar Bai, his own concubine (*haram*), that she may be exchanged [with Hira Bai]." And immediately afterwards he sent the aunt in a litter to the prince; when she objected saying that she would not go, he insisted, "Go quickly, if you love your life." So she had no help but to go and tell everything to the prince, who was highly pleased and cried out, "What of [giving him] one [inmate of my harem]? Immediately take with yourself in the *palki* in which you have come both of them, as I have no objection!" The aunt sent a report of the facts to her husband by means of an eunuch. Saif Khan said, "Now no cover is left [for me to take refuge in]," and mounted and sent the *Bai* to the prince without delay.

*Text.*—Ir. MS. 20*a*—21*a*.

*Notes.*—There are many mistakes in the above account. Saif Khan, who had married Malika Banu (not Saliha), the eldest sister of Mumtaz Mahal, was removed from the governorship of Khandesh at Shah Jahan's accession (1628) and never again employed there. Malika died on 25th August, 1641 (Ab. Hamid's *Pad.* ii. 241). Her husband, Saif Khan Mirza Safi (*M. U.* ii. 416—421), died in Bengal in May, 1640 (Ab. Hamid's *Pad.* ii. 198),

The following version of the episode given in the *Masir-ul-umara*, seems to be the correct one:—

Mir Khalil, (successively surnamed Muftakhar Khan, Sipahdar Khan, and Khan-i-Zaman), a son-in-law of Asaf Khan, was sent to the Deccan as Chief of the Artillery in the 23rd year of

Shah Jahan, 1649—50. (Text has 30th or 3rd year. Both dates wrong, *vide M. U.* iii. 501). In 1653, he became commandant of Dharur. It was only in Aurangzib's reign that he became subahdar of Khandesh [July 1681. Died July 1684. *(M.A.* 246)]. Zainabadi, who was beloved by Aurangzib before his accession, had been, it is said, in the Khan's harem as his concubine. One day the prince went with the ladies of his harem to the garden of Zainabad Burhanpur, named *Ahu-khanah* [Deer Park] and began to stroll with his chosen beloved ones. Zainabadi, whose musical skill ravished the senses, and who was unique in blandishments, having come in the train of Khan-i-Zaman's wife (the prince's maternal aunt), on seeing a fruit-laden mango-tree, in mirth and amorous play advanced, leaped up and plucked a fruit, without paying due respect to the prince's presence. This move of hers robbed the prince of his senses and self-control. With shameful importunity he procured her from his aunt's house, and became infatuated and given up to her, in spite of all his severe continence and temperance and pure training in theology. The story goes that one day she offered him a cup of wine and requested him to drink it. All his professions of reluctance and entreaty were disregarded. Then the poor prince was (at last) about to drink it, when that sly enchantress snatched away the cup (from his hand) and said 'My purpose was to test your love and not to embitter your mouth with this wicked and unlucky liquor!' This love-affair proceeded to such lengths as to reach Shah Jahan's ears. Dara Shukoh, who loved not Aurangzib, made capital of this incident to slander his brother to the Emperor, saying, 'See the piety and abstinence of this hypocritical knave! He has gone to the dogs for the sake of a wench of his aunt's household.' By chance the rose of her life withered in its very spring time, and left the prince seared with the brand of eternal separation. She is buried at Aurangabad close to the big tank. On the day of her death the prince became very unwell; in extreme agitation he rode out to hunt. Mir Askari (Aqil Khan), who was in attendance, secured a private audience and remonstrated, 'What wisdom is there in resolving to hunt in this (disturbed) state?' The prince replied, *(Verse)*

'Lamentation in the house cannot relieve the heart,
In solitude alone you can cry to your heart's content.'

Aqil Khan recited the following couplet [of his own composition] as apt for the occasion:

'How easy did love appear, but alas how hard it is!
How hard was separation, but what repose it gave to the beloved!'

The prince could not check his tears, but committed the verses to his memory, (*M.U.* i. 790-792) after vainly trying to learn the modest poet's name. (*Ibid.* ii. 823).

Manucci (i. 231) narrates the story thus:—

"Aurangzib grew very fond of one of the dancing-women in his harem, and through the great love he bore to her he neglected for some time his prayers and his austerities, filling up his days with music and dances; and going even farther, he enlivened himself with wine, which he drank at the instance of the said dancing-girl. The dancer died, and Aurangzib made a vow never to drink wine again nor to listen to music. In after-days he was accustomed to say that God had been very gracious to him by putting an end to that dancing-girl's life, by reason of whom he had committed so many iniquities, and had run the risk of never reigning through being occupied in vicious practices."

Now, when did the episode happen? Aurangzib was twice subahdar of the Deccan, *viz*, 1636—1644 and 1653—1657. It was only during the second of these periods that this Khan-i-Zaman, Murshid Quli Khan Khurasani (*M.U.* iii. 493), and Mir Askari served in the Deccan. Therefore, the date seems to have been 1653 at the earliest, when Aurangzib was 35 years old and the father of six children; he was not exactly a passionate youth who might consider the world well lost for love.

Akbar made it a rule that the concubines of the Mughal Emperors should be named after the places of their birth or the towns in which they were admitted to the harem. (Waris's *Padishahnamah*, 45*b*). Hence we have ladies surnamed Akbarabadi, Fathpuri, Aurangabadi, Zainabadi, and Udaipuri. Zainabad is the name of a suburb on the bank of the Tapti opposite Burhanpur. In Inayetullah's *Ahkam* (131*a*) our heroine's tomb is mentioned, though her name is wrongly spelt *Zainpuri*.

## §6. Aurangzib's precautions in beginning the War of Succession.

At the time when Aurangzib left Aurangabad in order to fight Dara Shukoh, and encamped at Arsul, four miles from the city, he ordered that there would be a halt of ten days there in order that his men might get their remaining needments ready. Nobody else durst remonstrate with him. Only Najabat Khan, who was a friend of firm fidelity and great boldness, said, "Stating the intention to march and then ordering a halt in this manner, will embolden the enemy." Aurangzib smiled and said, "First, tell me how they will be emboldened, and then I shall give you my answer." The Khan replied, "When the enemy will hear of our long halt here, they will send a strong force to bar our path." Aurangzib said, "That is the very essence of [my] policy. If I march quickly I shall have to encounter the whole army [of Dara at one place]. But if I delay here, my contest will be with the first division [of the enemy's] force. It is easier to defeat the first division than to defeat the whole army. In case he himself [*i.e.* Dara] has the boldness to advance and crosses the Narmada, his condition will be this: (*Verse*)

The man who goes far from his asylum and home
Becomes helpless, needy, and forsaken.
In the water even the lion becomes the prey of fishes,
On dry land the crocodile becomes the food of ants.

This delay is for the above purpose and not for whiling away my time. Nay more, there is another object, on which the advantage already mentioned is dependent. This second object is that I may know the circumstances of the men accompanying me, both poor and rich ; if a man delays in spite of his being well-to-do, then it is better not to take him along any farther from this place, because in future this circumstance will prove a source of utter weakness. In case I make a quick march, those nobles whose sincerity is doubtful may show negligence and delay, and then the distance [from my base] being great, it will be impossible to remedy the evil, and I shall have either to helplessly leave them defaulting or to return and correct them."

When Najabat Khan heard this, he kissed Aurangzib's feet and cried out, "**God knows best where to send one on a prophetic mission.**"

The above blessed saying was verified by this fact that Mirza Shah Nawaz Khan, one of the officers appointed to the Deccan, did not come* with Aurangzib during the first day's march, and on the second day's march, he submitted, "In consideration of my being a servant of Shah Jahan, I have no help but to remain here by resigning my military rank. I have no connection with Dara Shukoh. One of my daughters has been married to you and another to Murad Bakhsh. I have no relationship with Dara Shukoh which it might be necessary for me to respect. Your Highness knows well that I have not shown, in any battle or halt, any shortcoming or holding back which may be attributed to cowardice or disloyalty."

* Ir. MS. reads *came*.

Aurangzib replied, "Indeed, the requisites of fidelity to salt are not distant from men of pure blood [like you]. But I am making some days' halt here; I wish to see you [daily] for some days, and shall give you leave to depart when I resume my march. What need is there that you should turn a private person (*faqir*) ?" Shah Nawaz Khan said, "This, too, is opposed to a servant's duties. This hereditary servant has set his heart on the work of the Emperor Shah Jahan."

After this Aurangzib gave out that he was down with looseness of the bowels. The nobles who came to pay the [customary] visit to the sick, were ordered to enter alone and one by one, leaving their attendants outside. Thus, on the second day, when Mirza Shah Nawaz Khan came, Shaikh Mir promptly arrested him, tied him hand and neck, and placed him handcuffed and fettered on the *hawda* of an elephant. That very moment Aurangzib gave the order to march. After reaching Burhanpur, Shah Nawaz Khan was thrown into prison. After the victory over Dara Shukoh, at the entreaty of Zeb-un-nisa Begam,—who had refused food for three days, saying that she would keep fasting till her maternal grandfather was released,—Aurangzib in anger and displeasure ordered him to be set free and appointed him governor of Ahmadabad, which province had been without a governor since Murad Bakhsh left it. But Aurangzib said, "My mind is not reassured [ about him ]. I have issued this order as I could not help it, but I shall reconsider it carefully afterwards. As he is a Sayyid, it is hard to order his execution. Otherwise, there is the well-known saying, 'A severed head tells no tale.' "

What he had said did finally come to pass. After Dara's flight, the Khan joined him in the battle of Ajmir and was slain in the midst of the fight.

*Text.*—Ir. Ms. 25*a*—26*b*.

*Notes.*—Aurangzib started from Aurangabad on 5th February, 1658 to contest the throne. At Arsul, 4 miles n.e. of the city, he halted for one day only. (*Alamgirnamah*, 43-44). But a halt of one month (18th Feb. —20th March) was made at Burhanpur. "Shah Nawaz Khan Safawi did not accompany Aurangzib, but lingered at Burhanpur under various pretexts. So the prince on reaching Mandua (25th March) sent Muhammad Sultan and Shaikh Mir back to Burhanpur to arrest and confine Shah Nawaz Khan in the fort of Burhanpur." (*Ibid.* 52). Shah Nawaz Khan Safawi, the father-in-law of Aurangzib, was a Sayyid of very high pedigree. (Life in *M. U.* ii. 670). At the end of September Aurangzib from Multan ordered his release and appointed him subahdar of Gujrat. Slain in the battle of Ajmir, 14th March, 1659. (*A. N.* 209, 323).

## § 7. Battle of Khajwa.

In the night preceding the day which had been fixed for the battle with Shuja, when about 7½ hours of the night had worn on, the Emperor learnt that Rajah Jaswant Singh, who had been given the command of the Vanguard, had determined to go over to Shuja with his own troops who numbered 14,000 cavalry and infantry, and that during his journey he had laid a severe hand on (*i. e.* looted) the followers and animals of the imperial camp, so that the orderly arrangement of the army had been broken up, and a great panic had seized the men, many of whom had joined that wretch's (Jaswant's) force and were advancing with him in the path of misfortune. The Emperor was then engaged in the *tahajjud* prayer ; on hearing the report he made a sign with his hand [as if to say] 'If he has gone away, let him go away,' but gave no other reply. After finishing his prayer, he summoned Mir Jumla and said, "This incident, too, is a mercy from God, for if the hypocrite had taken this step in the midst of the battle, it would have been hard to remedy the mischief."

Then he ordered the kettledrums to be beaten and his mount to be got ready. Riding an elphant, he passed the rest of the night in that condition.

When the sun rose it was found that the army of Shuja was coming on from the left side firing its artillery. * A number of men, whose day of death had arrived, were slain. Aurangzib ordered the driver of his elephant, "Make my elephant reach Shuja's elephant by any means that you can." Just then Murshid Quli Khan, who was the Emperor's counsellor and close companion, said, "This kind of audacity is opposed to the practice of emperors." Aurangzib replied, "Neither of us has yet become emperor. Men become emperors only after showing this sort of daring. And if after one has become emperor his courage decreases, his authority does not last. (*Verse*)

"That man [alone] can tightly clasp in his arms the bride of kingship
Who plants kisses on the keen sword's lip."

*Text.*—Ir. MS. 4*b*—5*a* ; MS. N. 33*a*—34*b*.

*Notes.*—The battle of Khajwa took place on 5th January,

---

* MS. N. reads differently : "It was found that the force with Aurangzib was not even one-fourth of Shuja's army. There was a short artillery-fight. He (Shuja) came on from the left side with his own vanguard."

1659, and ended in the utter rout of Shuja. For a full account of the battle see *History of Aurangzib*, ch. 19. Murshid Quli Khan, Khurasani, (*Masir-ul-umara*, iii. 493—500), the able revenue administrator of the Deccan during Aurangzib's viceroyalty, was slain in the battle of Dharmat, and so could not have been present at Khajwa. The other Murshid Quli Khan, Nawab of Bengal, entered the imperial service long afterwards. *Tahajjud*, the last prayer of the night, is usually said after midnight.

## § 8. Aurangzib's last will and testament.

**"Praise be to God and blessing on those servants [ of Him ] who have become sanctified and have given satisfaction [ to Him ].** I have some [instructions to leave as my] last will and testament:

FIRST,—On behalf of this sinner sunk in iniquity [*i. e.* myself] cover [with an offering of cloth and carpet] the holy tomb of Hasan **(on him be peace !)**, because those who are drowned in the ocean of sin have no other protection except seeking refuge with that Portal of Mercy and Forgiveness. The means of performing this greatly auspicious act are with my noble son, Prince Alijah [ Md. Azam ]; take them.

SECOND,—Four Rupees and two annas, out of the price of the caps sewn by me, are with Aia Bega, the *mahaldar*. Take the amount and spend it on the shroud of this helpless creature. Three hundred and five Rupees, from the wages of copying the Quran, are in my purse for personal expenses. Distribute them to the faqirs on the day of my death. As the money got as by copying the Quran is regarded by the Shia sect as illegal, do not spend it on my shroud and other necessaries.

THIRD,—Take the remaining necessaries [of my

funeral] from the agent of Prince Alijah; as he is the nearest heir among my sons, and on him lies the responsibility for the lawful or unlawful [practices at my funeral]; this helpless person (*i. e.*, Aurangzib) is not answerable for them, because the dead are in the hands of the survivors.

FOURTH,—Bury this wanderer in the Valley of Deviation from the Right Path with his head bare, because every ruined sinner who is conducted bare-headed before the Grand Emperor (*i.e.*, God), is sure to be an object of mercy.

FIFTH,—Cover the top of the coffin on my bier with the coarse white cloth called *gazi*. Avoid the spreading of a canopy and uncanonical innovations like [processions of] musicians and the celebration of the Prophet's Nativity (*maulud*).

SIXTH,—It is proper for the ruler of the kingdom (*i.e.*, my heir) to treat kindly the helpless servants who in the train of this shameless sinner [Aurangzib] have been roving in the deserts and wilderness [of the Deccan]. Even if any manifest fault is committed by them, give them in return for it gracious forgiveness and benign overlooking [of the fault].

SEVENTH,—No other nation is better than the Persians for acting as accountants (*mutasaddi*). And in war, too, from the age of the Emperor Humayun to the present time, none of this nation has turned his face away from the field, and their firm feet have never been shaken. Moreover, they have not once been guilty of disobedience or treachery to their master. But, as they insist on being treated with great honour, it is very difficult to get on together with them. You have anyhow to conciliate them, and should employ subterfuges.

EIGHTH,—The Turani people have ever been soldiers. They are very expert in making charges, raids, night-attacks and arrests. They feel no suspicion, despair or shame when commanded to make a retreat in the very midst of a fight, which means, in other words, 'drawing the arrow back';—and they are a hundred stages remote from the crass stupidity of the Hindustanis, who would part with their heads but not leave their positions [in battle]. In every way, you should confer favours on this race, because on many occasions these men can do the necessary service, when no other race can.

NINTH,—You should treat the Sayyids of Barha, who are worthy of blessing, according to the Quranic verse, **'Give unto the near relations [of the Prophet] their dues,'** and never grow slack in honouring and favouring them. Inasmuch as, according to the blessed verse, **'I say I do not ask of you any recompense for it except love to [my] kinsmen'**, love for this family is **the wages of [Muhammad's] Prophetship,** you should never be wanting [in respect for them], and it will be fruitful of benefit in this world and the next. But you should be extremely cautious in dealing with the Sayyids of Barha. Be not wanting in love of them at heart, but externally do not increase their rank, because they become predominant partners in the government, nay more, they would demand the kingdom for themselves. If you let them take the reins ever so little, the result will be your own disgrace.

TENTH,—As far as possible the ruler of a kingdom

should not spare himself from moving about; he should avoid staying in one place, which outwardly gives him repose but in effect brings on a thousand calamities and troubles.

ELEVENTH,—Never trust your sons, nor treat them during your lifetime in an intimate manner, because, if the Emperor Shah Jahan had not treated Dara Shukoh in this manner, his affairs would not have come to such a sorry pass. Ever keep in view the saying, 'The words of a king are barren.'

TWELFTH,—The main pillar of government is to be well informed in the news of the kingdom. Negligence for a single moment becomes the cause of disgrace for long years. The escape of the wretch Shiva took place through [my] carelessness, and I have to labour hard [against the Marathas] to the end of my life, [as the result of it].

Twelve is blessed [among numbers]. I have concluded with twelve directions. (*Verse*)

It you learn [the lesson], a kiss on your wisdom,
If you neglect it, then alas! alas!"

*Text.*—Ir. MS. 8*b*—10*a*. MS. N. 1*b*—3*b* is incomplete and ends with the 9th clause.

## SECTION II.

## ABOUT HIS SONS AND GRANDSONS

### A. BAHADUR SHAH (MUAZZAM).

### § 9. Arrest of Prince Muazzam.

WHEN the Emperor called for Prince Muhammad Muazzam Bahadur Shah, intending to imprison him, he came to the Emperor in the chapel. His Majesty told Bakhtawar Khan, the Superintendent of the Perfumery Department, "Bring every essence (*atar*) that my son wishes for." Bahadur Shah submitted, "What power has this slave to make any choice himself? Any essence that your Majesty may be graciously pleased to present would be better [than one of my selection]." The Emperor replied, "This order of mine is also an act of grace." Then Bahadur Shah told Bakhtawar Khan, "Any essence that you have except the essence of scented wax (*atar-i-fitna*), is good." His Majesty cried out, "Yes, I too, having the same prudential consideration in my mind, have troubled you to come to this house." When the essence arrived, he ordered the prince to put off his arms and come nearer, in order that the Emperor might, with his own hand, rub him over with the essence. After the perfuming, when the prince went [back] to make his bow (of thanksgiving), the Emperor went away, ordering Muharram Khan with the help of Hamid-ud-din Khan, to disarm the four sons of the prince, and detain all the five there. As they went up first of all to Muhammad Muiz-ud-din, the latter laid his hand on the hilt of his sword. Bahadur Shah in anger cried out [to his son], "Wretch, you are resisting the order of your Centre of Faith and K'aba (*i.e.*, His Sacred Majesty) !" With his own hands he tore off his [eldest] son's arms and gave them up to Muharram Khan. The other sons without objection stripped off their arms and surrendered them.

When the Emperor heard of it, he said, "The chapel has taken the place of the Well of Joseph, and he will attain to the dignity of Joseph."

*Text.*—Ir. MS 7*a*.

*Notes.*—Prince Muazzam, afterwards Emperor Bahadur Shah I., was imprisoned by Aurangzib on 21st February, 1687, and released on 9th May, 1695, when he was sent to Lahor as governor. The *Masir-i-Alamgiri* (p. 291) gives a slightly different account of the manner of his arrest. The Bakhtawar Khan of this anecdote could not have been the author of the *Mirat-i-alam* (who died on 9th February, 1695), but was evidently Khwajah Bakhtawar, created a Khan in April, 1705. There is a play upon the word *fitna*, which means (1) scented wax and (2) disturbance, tumult. The Kaba is the square temple of black stone at Mecca, towards which Muslims turn their faces when praying. Joseph, the son of Jacob, was flung into a dry well by his wicked brothers, and then sold as a slave to some merchants going to Egypt, and this calamity was the means of his future greatness as the prime-minister of Egypt. (*Genesis*, xxxvii. 24.)

## § 10 Wise Counsels for Kings.

On the day when the Emperor released Bahadur Shah from captivity, he made him sit down in his presence and told him, "As a father like me has been pleased with you, the crown will certainly fall to your lot. I had no need to satisfy [*my* father] Shah Jahan, as he was devoted to Dara Shukoh, who had become an unbeliever through the companionship of Hindus and *yogis* (ascetics). It is simply the assistance of the faith of the Sayyid among Prophets, *i.e.*, Muhammad, **(on whom be blessings and peace !)** that is the cause of victory. * Some counsels I am going to give you ; you should lay them to heart. Although I know it for certain that it is far from your nature to put them into practice, yet I am speaking out of paternal affection and in view of the love and obedience which you have shown.

"FIRST,—an Emperor ought to stand midway between gentleness and severity. If either of these two qualities exceeds the other, it becomes a cause of the ruin of his throne, because in case of excessive gentleness the people display audacity, while the increase of harshness scares away hearts, *e.g.*, my uncle Sultan Ulugh Beg, in spite of his graces and good qualities, was fearless in shedding blood, so that for petty offences he used to order executions. His son, Abdul Latif, made him prisoner and sent him to the fort of Nehawand. On the way he asked a man, 'What do you think was the cause of the fall of my royal power ?' The man answered, 'On account of your bloodshed, which made men shrink from you.' What my august ancestor the Emperor Humayun displayed was improper negligence, forgiveness, and weakness in affairs, because, in spite of his repeatedly hearing of the audacious deeds of Sher Khan in the province of Bengal, he neglected [Sher Khan], and only rebuked his father, Hasan Sur, saying, 'You know of your son's acts and yet you do not write to him [to

* Text has 'advice' which makes no sense. I read *nusrat* for *nasihat*.

remonstrate] !' Hasan replied, 'His acts have passed beyond the stage of writing. I know not what your Majesty's negligence will at last result in.'

"NEXT this,—an Emperor should never allow himself to be fond of ease and inclined to retirement, because the most fatal cause of the decline of kingdoms and the destruction of royal power is this undesirable habit. Always be moving about, as much as possible. (*Verse*)

It is bad for both emperors and water to remain at the same place,
The water grows putrid and the king's power slips out of his control.
In touring lie the honour, ease, and splendour of kings,
The desire of comfort and happiness makes them untrustworthy.

"NEXT this,—always plan how to train your servants, and appoint every one to the task for which you deem him fit. It is opposed to wisdom to order a carpet-weaver to do the work of blacksmith. Don't impose the task of the great on the small, nor that of the little on the great, because great people feel ashamed in doing the work of small men, and little fellows have not the capacity for doing the work of the great, so that utter disorder prevails in the affairs of the State."

*Text.*—Ir. MS. 7a—8a.

*Notes.*—Mirza Ulugh Beg, a grandson of Timur, and the learned author of Astronomical Tables, was king of Samarqand till 1449, when he was deposed and murdered by his son Abdul Latif.

## § 11. Advice to his Heir. Gloomy Prophecy.

When the Emperor released Prince Muhammad Muazzam Bahadur Shah from confinement, he conferred favours and gifts on him, and, on the day of giving him leave to depart, said, "Although out of sheer necessity and because I had no other choice, I have punished your extremely ruinous conduct by keeping you in prison for some years, yet, this is the strongest sign of [your future] kingship, as the throne and dignity of Joseph were dependent on his being [first] imprisoned. God willing, the same will happen to you. In this hope I have in my lifetime entrusted to you [the governorship of] paradise-like Hindustan.

"The presages of my horoscope,—composed by Fazil Khan Ala-ul-mulk, [and giving the incidents] from the day of my birth till after my death,—have all been verified by actual experience.* In that horoscope it is written that after me † will come an Emperor, ignorant, narrow-minded, overpowered by injuries,—whose words will be all imperfect and whose plans will be all immature. He will act towards some men with so much prodigality as almost to drown them, and towards others with so much rigour as to raise the fear of [utter] destruction. All these admirable qualities and praiseworthy characteristics are found

---

* One example of the correctness of the horoscope is given in *Masir-ul-umara*, iii. 529.

† The translation here follows the Ir. MS. But MS. N. reads, "After this reign, which is the divider of the life of *Samak-i-ramih* and *Samak-i-a'zal* (two portions of the constellation Leo) and is situated at the most conspicuous place of the degree of ascendency, an Emperor shall come, &c."

in your nature! Although I shall send [? or leave] behind me a competent *wazir* who has come to the front in my reign and whom I have secured, yet what good will it do, as the four pillars of the empire, *viz.* my four sons, will never leave that poor man to himself to do his work? In spite of this being the case, [he] will still exert [himself] so that the work [of administration] will on the whole be well done. But it is a rule of medicine that although the lower limbs of the body may retain their strength so long as the bad humour does not descend from the upper parts of the body, in the end the disease turns into [general] weakness and slackness, nay even into disorder and death. In this matter, too, the same is the case. Although owing to my marching through wildernesses and forests, my officers, who love repose and feel disgusted with their own parents, long for the destruction of this my borrowed life,—yet after my death they will, owing to the thoughtlessness and ignorance of this son incapable of appreciating merit, beg from God for themselves that very thing (*viz.*, death) which they are now praying for me. Any how, I advise you, out of fatherly love, 'Don't be so salt that [your subjects] would spit you out of their mouths, nor be so sweet that they may gulp you down.' But this advice is out of place here, as saltishness is not at all present in your nature, but is the share of your dear brother. The portion of saltlessness is the lot of you, my very sagacious son. May God keep both the brothers in perfect moderation! Amen, O Lord of the Universe!"

*Text.*—Ir. MS. 19*b* & 20*a*, MS. N. 21*b*—23*a*.

*Notes.*—Aurangzib's last and most favourite *wazir* was

Asad Khan. Fazil Khan (Mulla Ala-ul-mulk Tuni), a versatile scholar, was Shah Jahan's *Khan-i-saman*. (Life in *M. U.* iii. 524—530).

## § 12. Infringement of Royal Prerogative.

From the news-letter of Kabul the Emperor learnt that Prince Muhammad Muazzam had at the time of holding Court ordered four drums to be beaten. The Emperor wrote, "The prime-minister should write to the prince a 'Letter By order' to this effect :—In the place of four drums you should beat four tabors, because it is the prerogative of Emperors alone to beat kettledrums while holding Court. When God gives you [the throne], you will [enjoy these imperial rights]. Why this impatience ?"

*Text.*—Ir. MS. 3*b*. MS. N. 9*b*-10*a*.

*Notes.*—Prince Muazzam ascended the throne as Bahadur Shah I. in 1707. He was appointed by his father subahdar of Afghanistan in May. 1698.

## § 13. Infringement of Royal Prerogative.

From the letter of the spy of the province of Afghanistan, the Emperor learnt that Prince Muhammad Muazzam Bahadur Shah performed the traditional prayers after setting up canvas screens (*kanat*) in the Jama Mosque. On the sheet of the letter Aurangzib wrote, "Verily this matter is not unconnected with fear and cowardice, which are traits of this son's character. In spite of such cowardice, he ought to have a little fear of *me*, too. How did he dare do a thing which is the special prerogative of kings ? The late Emperor Shah Jahan was negligent towards his sons, so that matters came to a pass that is notorious." On the margin the Emperor wrote, "The *nazir* (of Kabul) is dismissed from his post and reduced in rank by a hundred troopers, as he has not written a single syllable about this affair. Muharram Khan should recommend another *nazir*. Entirely change the *jagirs* of the news-writer and reporter [of Kabul]. I have not degraded them in rank as they may be of service in future. The spy should quickly make another inquiry and report the facts. If it is true, the prince should be removed from the governorship and summoned to my presence."

*Text.*—Ir. MS. 10*a* & *b*., not in MS. N.

## § 14. Royal Prerogative infringed.

The Emperor learnt from the letter of the *nazir* of Muhammad Muazzam Bahadur Shah that when the prince was issuing from the *chakla* of Sarhind he whispered something into the ears of the superintendent of the elephants which the writer could not catch. When they had marched 8 miles from the [last] halting place, a fight took place between two infuriated elephants. The prince himself stopped with his troops and camp-followers and witnessed the fight ; afterwards the drivers of the two elephants separated them from each other and continued the journey. But in this combat neither of the elephants had hurt or trodden down any person.

On the sheet the Emperor wrote, "The first statement was due to fear for his own life, as concealment [of the matter] was not possible. The second correction, *viz*. that 'neither of the elephants had hurt anybody,' displays the shame of avarice which makes people blind and dumb. The chief paymaster should reduce the *nazir's* rank by 200 and change his *jagir* in proportion to the reduction in his rank. The prime-minister should write to the foolish prince a 'Letter by Order' instead of a *farman*. saying, Ordering an elephant-fight is the exclusive prerogative of kings. By these useless and unprofitable longings you cannot get the crown sooner. When the time comes and it is in your destiny, you will be king. What ruins a man is demanding more than his lot and before the ordained time. Why do you [by such assumption of royalty] make me angry and yourself afflicted ?"

*Text.*—Ir. MS. 11*a* & *b* ; MS. N. 21*a* & *b*.

## § 15. Royal Prerogative Infringed.

From the news-letter of the province of Kabul the Emperor learnt that Muhammad Muazzam Bahadur Shah, on the days that he held Court, used to sit on a platform erected one yard above the ground. The Emperor wrote on the sheet, [*Verse*]

"It is not by mere wishing that our works are done.
God's grace is required in every work.
You cannot secure the seat of great ones by [mere] rash acts.
Unless you have gathered together all the materials for greatness.

It is very strange that the confinement of so many years has not reformed the presumptuous mind of this proud and foolish [prince]. Two strict mace-bearers should be sent to make him get down from his seat in open Court, and to dismantle the platform. If they arrive [at Kabul] when he is not holding Court, they should wait till he does so, and then carry out my order. **as a recompense for that which they do.** The late

Emperor Shah Jahan showed so much carelessness and negligence towards his sons that the independent chief of affairs was turned upside down."

*Text.*—Ir. MS. 2*b*.

## § 16. Suspicious watching of his sons.

Hamida Banu, the superintendent (*mahaldar*) of the harem of Muhammad Muazzam Bahadur Shah, from the province of Multan petitioned the Emperor, "Very often at night in the prince's private chamber, where his beloved ones come, he takes with himself his pen-case and memorandum-book. Out of regard for etiquette it is not allowed by the Court regulations that the *mahaldar* or her deputy should be present at that time. When your Majesty gave this old slave woman [the writer] her congee you told her orally, and you also inserted it in a [subsequent] royal letter, that whenever the prince would call for his pen-case this old bondmaid or her deputy Sharf-un-nisa should be present. These are the facts. What order in this matter?"

The Emperor wrote in answer, "If you cannot in etiquette go to the prince's private chamber, what etiquette is there in your refusing to send him the pen-case? In any case in future do not at all leave the pen-case in the inner apartments. I have also sent an order to the *nazir* that whenever the prince in the outer apartments needs [writing materials] he should produce the pen-case, so that the prince may keep it with himself only till the necessary signatures are finished; thereafter the *nazir* should keep it under his own seal. The *nazir* should tell my foolish son that his captivity for so many years has not made him wise, as he has taken such audacious steps! Even now the matter has not gone out [of my hand]. Distance cannot prevent [me from] punishing [him]. (*Verse*)

> Here is the polo-ball, and here is the field,
> You inconsiderate, utterly ignorant man."

*Text.*—MS. N. 20*a* 6—20*b* 12.

*Notes.*—Prince Muazzam after having been confined by his father from 1687, was finally released in 1695, and on 13th July. 1696, went to Multan as governor, (*M. A.* 382). Here he remained for two years, nominally a viceroy, but still watched by his jealous father's spies. The *mahaldar* was the highest female servant and controlled the harem,—a sort of female *major domo.* She evidently acted as a spy in the interests of the Emperor.

B. Azam Shah

## § 17. The Capitulation of Parli.

The siege of the fort of Parli had continued for four months, and then the rainy season approached. It was usual in that part for the rains to be accompanied by hail-storms. The soldiers were in consequence greatly alarmed. Shaikh Sadullah Khan submitted to the Emperor, through Muharram Khan, "If the Emperor's son Alijah would not be displeased, peace can be made in a day." His Majesty said, "Wait to-day; the answer will be given to-morrow." In the evening it became known that the prince had an intolerable aversion to making peace, and that the Shaikh had arranged for the surrender of the fort on the sole condition that the commandant and the garrison should go out [freely] without any property. The Emperor said, "Make the agreement complete, so that immediately on my giving the order, the imperial flag may be planted on the fort without any delay." As he ordered, the settlement was made firm.

Next day, when holding the morning Court, His Majesty said to Prince Alijah, "I have to show consideration for your feelings. Otherwise, making peace is not so very difficult. Others, too, may accomplish it." The prince replied, "I agree to any method by which your Majesty's work can be done." The Emperor rejoined, "But you will afterwards feel aggrieved !" The prince answered, "What power has this slave to be displeased with his holy guide and preceptor ?" and then [after a pause] he asked, "Who is this man, the mediator in making peace ?" "Shaikh Sadullah" answered His Majesty. The prince said, "Let the order be issued." As Shaikh Sadullah was not present at Court, the Emperor told Muharram Khan, "Send word to the Shaikh to plant the flag quickly on the fort." After two *gharis* the flag was set up there and the music of victory was played. Prince Azam with extreme irritation and roughness said, "We servants of your Majesty ought now to take poison, as these rascals (*paji*) have become your counsellors." The Emperor answered, "I have indeed cherished rascals. Now I shall drive both the rascals out of my camp. Shaikh Sadullah will be sent to the Base Camp, and you to the province of Ahmadabad (*i.e.*, Gujrat)." Then he ordered that Siadat Khan, the superintendent of the mace-bearers, with all the mace-bearers should accompany the prince and make him dismount at Sanpgaon, 3 *koses* from the imperial army, without permitting the prince to go back to his present quarters. Then His Majesty dropped the screen and rose from the Court. Prince Azam, in confusion and bewilderment, entreated the mediation of Asad Khan, the *wazir*, who begged the Emperor to give the prince two days' respite, that the rains might stop a little. His Majesty replied, "What business have my servants to say anything in the affairs of my sons ?" Asad Khan felt ashamed of having made the request. Eventually the prince went with the superintendent of the mace-bearers, took up his residence in the camp at Sanpgaon, and thence submitted to the Emperor, "Wax for making oil-cloth cannot be had." Aurangzib replied, "You may take some from the imperial Government [stores] after paying the price." The prince prayed that the price might be deducted from his cash stipend. The Emperor wrote [on the application],—"No wise man leaves cash for credit, * for at the time of payment who knows who will be alive and who will be dead ? You must pay the price in cash and take [the wax]." So, the prince did as he was ordered; he sent Rs. 1,200 and got the wax.

*Text.*—Ir. MS. 2*a*—3*a*, MS. N. 39*a*—40*b*.

*Notes.*—The fort of Parli, 4 m. from Satara, was besieged by Aurangzib from 30th April to 9th June, 1700 (*Masir-i-Alamgiri*, 425—428). Prince Alijah was Muhammad Azam, the 3rd son of Aurangzib. Shaikh Sadullah was at one time the *mushrif* of the Emperor's personal attendants (*khawas*). Mace-bearers were sergeants who made arrests and carried out the Emperor's disciplinary orders.

---

* MS. N. reads. "It can't be. This is credit business, while I have written about cash payment. When the time for paying [the credit price] comes, there is no knowing &c."

## § 18. Strict Justice between a Prince and a Commoner

Prince Muhammad Azam Shah wrote a letter to Inayetullah Khan with instructions to submit to the Emperor the purport of the letter and his requests. He stated therein, "Sayyid L'al, who has been holding a rank (*mansab*) in the imperial service for three generations, drinks wine and does many kinds of irreligious practices (*bid'at*) in my *jagir* of Mandesor. The Emperor should order his *jagir* to be taken away from him and given to me, so that this evil may be put down." The Emperor wrote across the petition,—"It is a novel and funny manner of appropriation to take on yourself a work which appertains to the Censor of Morals and to pray for the transfer of another's *jagir*. It is impossible to transfer a *jagir* held for one generation only,—not to speak of one enjoyed for three generations. Nobody's *jagir* is transferred at the mere word of another man. In being my servants this son and Sayyid L'al are exactly equal, while the latter, by reason of his being a Sayyid, is a thousand steps higher. The chief *Sadar* should write to the Censor of that place to enquire into the truth of the matter and report the details to me. Praised be God that I have not given my sons predominance as the Emperor Shah Jahan did, lest I should be put to disgrace [by them]."

*Text.*—Ir. MS. 3*a*—3*b*, MS. N. 8*b*—9*a* incomplete and confused.

*Note.*—Censor of Morals or *Muhtasib*, an officer appointed to see that the ordinances of Islam are strictly observed in private life. [See my *Mughal Administration*, 2nd ed., ch. 2. § 8.]

## § 19. Be not too bold.

The Emperor learnt from the news-letter of the army of Prince Muhammad Azam Shah that he used to go incautiously towards the entrenchments in order to view the fort of Panhala. Although the *nazir* and the *mahaldar* forbade him, he did not mind their prohibition. The same thing was also reported to the Emperor in the letters of the *nazir* and the *mahaldar*.

His Majesty wrote, "I wonder at this son, on whom my society has produced no [educative] effect whatever! He is a thousand stages remote from caution and far-sightedness, and has not laid to heart the maxim **'Precaution is a suspicion of mischief,'** nor put to use the verse **'Don't thrust yourself with your own hands into destruction.'** (*Verses*)

A bird that is prudent in this garden of a world,
Suspects the rose of being the claws of a royal falcon!
When a partridge flies without circumspection,
Blood drops from its visible wounds, as the result of its laughter.
The society of the good does not turn a bad nature into good,
The almond comes out of sugar as bitter as before.

Manliness does not consist in audacity and recklessness, but in breaking one's self (*i.e.*, humility). (*Verses*)

The perfection of manliness and humanity lies in self-suppression.
Kiss the hand of the man who has broken this bow (*i.e.*, self)."

*Text.*—Ir. MS. 18*a*—*b*.

*Notes.*—Panhala, 11 m. s. w. of Kolhapur. Aurangzib captured it after a siege lasting from 9th March to 28th May, 1701. (*Masir-i-Alamgiri*, 430—439; Khafi Khan, ii. 476—490).

## § 20. Prince Azam punished for quarrelling with the Superintendent of his harem.

Bahroz Khan, the *nazir* of the *deorhi* of Prince Muhammad Azam Shah, reported to the Emperor, "The prince has behaved badly towards Nur-un-nisa, the *mahaldar*, as he did not take her with himself [in his visit] to the imperial garden at Ahmadabad. The *mahaldar* sent a letter outside [the harem to me] forbidding the prince's journey. So, this slave (*i.e.*, the writer) came and stopped the riding out of the prince, in the absence of any order [from the Emperor]. The prince expelled the *mahaldar* from his assembly (*majlis*)." The Emperor wrote this order :—"The *mansabdars* appointed [to that province] and Khwajah Quli Khan with his own troops and the Rajah of Narwar, should co-operate and prevent the prince from riding out or giving audience, pending the arrival of order from me."

Next day, when the prince got news of it, he sent a petition through his sister, Padishah Begam, begging pardon for his offences, and enclosing an agreement to a compromise sealed with the seals of the *nazir* and the *mahaldar*. On the petition the Emperor wrote :—"I refrain from transferring your *mahals* (*i.e.*, *jagir*). But if no pecuniary punishment is inflicted, you will retain the audacity to do this sort of work again. Fifty thousand Rupees should be taken from the cash salary of this short-sighted, base-minded and foolish son, into the public treasury as punishment for this offence."

*Text.*—Ir. MS. 4*a* & *b*, MS. N. 5*a* & *b*.

*Notes.*—Prince Azam was subahdar of Gujrat from the

middle of 1701 to November, 1705. Padishah Begam was the title of his sister Zinat-un-nisa.

## § 21. Maintain peace on the highways.

From the report of the province of Ahmadabad, of which Muhammad Azam Shah was the governor, the Emperor learnt—"Janaji Dalia, a commander of the enemy [*i.e.*, Marathas], had plundered some merchants on the highway of Surat, at a place 80 miles from Ahmadabad. This matter had become known to Shah Alijah [*i.e.*, Azam] from a news-letter; but he had said, 'It has occurred within the *faujdari* of Amanat Khan, the collector of Surat; I have no concern with it'."

On the sheet of the report the Emperor wrote,—"Decrease five thousand from the substantive rank of the prince, and take from his agents money corresponding to the [loss] reported by the merchants. If it had been an officer other than a prince, this order would have been issued after an inquiry. For a prince the punishment is the absence of investigation. Bravo for your princeship, that you consider yourself lower than Amanat Khan! As in my lifetime you are claiming to inherit the empire, why then do you not make Amanat Khan a sharer of your heritage during my life? (*Verse*)

A malady that does not go away for medicine, has no cure.
A man who has no wisdom, does not need any thing."

*Text.*—Ir. MS. 22*b*, MS. N. 26*b*—27*a*.

*Note.*—Dalia is probably Dalway, a Maratha family name.

## § 22. Unintentional contempt of "Court" punished.

One day when the Emperor was holding Court,

Prince Muhammad Azam Shah stood up and made a request. At not getting a reply favourable to his desire, he grew angry and advanced so far that his foot touched the Emperor's seat (*masnad*). The Emperor in displeasure dropped the screen of the Court, went away, and forbade the prince to come to the presence. Nobody else had the power to intercede with him; but Shah Salimullah, [a hermit] of Nandurbar, said to the Emperor, "That the prince advanced his foot was not due to a spirit of daring, but to carelessness. **Of him who pardons and makes peace, the recompense is from God.**" Below the above [Quranic] verse the Emperor wrote,— (*Verse*)

"From the bank of safety into the sea of destruction, fell
That man who set his steps beyond his own limits."

*Text.*—Ir. MS. 5*b*, MS. N. 32*a* & *b*.

*Note.*—When the Emperor dropped a screen in front of his seat at a *darbar*, it was a sign that the Court was closed. Then he retired to the *harem* by a door at the back of his seat.

## § 23. The Emperor's repartee.

Prince Muhammad Azam Shah, owing to his levity of character and vileness of tongue, had likened His Majesty to the sweeper Jama who used to serve in the Hall of Private Audience, and the matter had reached the imperial ears. One day, while Jama was sweeping the courtyard of the Private Audience Hall, the Emperor turned towards Azam Shah and said, "Baba! this sweeper has four sons." Azam Shah replied, "He has only one son, and that too a mere child." His Majesty rejoined, "Your statement is wrong. My information is even that one of these four sons has gone away to Persia!" On hearing these words, the prince understood the point [of the Emperor's speech] and was greatly ashamed. He complained to his sister, Zinat-un-nisa Begam, "His Majesty, utterly disregarding the consideration and honour due to my lady mother, has described Jama sweeper as my father!" The Emperor retorted, "But, then, son! you showed no consideration and honour to Shah Jahan, when you described his late Majesty's son as the sweeper Jama!"

*Text.*—Ir. MS. 6*a*, MS. N. 11*a* & *b*.

*Note.*—Only four sons of Aurangzib were alive at this time, and one of these, Prince Akbar, had fled to Persia after the failure of his rebellion in 1681.

## § 24. Aurangzib keeps his sons at a distance.

Muhammad Azam Shah, who was governor of Gujrat, petitioned thus,—"On account of the length of my illness, which was a quartan fever for a long time—though the disease has been totally removed for more than two months, I am still so weak that I cannot utter words. I pray for a transfer from this province to the Emperor's presence, so that at all events I may, after attaining the blessing of kissing the Emperor's feet, give up my weak life."

The Emperor wrote, "May the True Protector watch over this fruit of my heart [=son] in all conditions! To allow you to travel and come to me in this state of weakness, would not be free from cruelty. (*Verse*)

He considers remembrance as higher than interview,
Thank God! my eyes are not ungrateful.

This weak old man and this shrunken helpless creature [Aurangzib] is afflicted with a hundred maladies besides anxiety [lit., headache], but he has made patience his habit. (*Verse*)

In the opinion of those who are ready for death,
Every unseasonable trouble sent by Fate appears as a suitable favour.

I have no greed for disease, otherwise
Every disease allotted to me is a medicine from the Invisible.

While talking with my wicked and reprehensible passions, I say that with the exception of the heart, which is precious and worth protecting, the world and everything in it deserve to be left behind. Why have you bound [yourself] to the world and temporal things? Your heart is to be taken [with you to the next world], and the World and Time will have to be given up. (*Verse*)

Every [earthly] thing which you elevate will throw you down into the dust.
Except the flow of tears, which is capable of elevating you [to heaven]."

*Text.*—MS. N. 10*a* 5—10*b* 11.

*Notes.*—In April, 1693, Prince Azam at Cuddapah in Madras had a long and severe attack of dropsy, after which he was conveyed to the Court by order of the Emperor, arriving there on 22nd October, 1693, (*M.A.* 353, 361—363 ; Khafi Khan, ii. 434). But he was *not* then governor of Gujrat. Khafi Khan gives the following account of an application made by the prince in 1705 to come from Gujrat and visit his father :—

"Prince Muhammad Azam, in Gujrat, on hearing of his father's illness, applied for permission to come to Court on the plea of the air and water of that province not being congenial to him. The Emperor was displeased and sent him a letter to this effect:—'I, too, had sent a similar petition to my father Shah Jahan during his illness [at the close of his reign], and he had replied to it by saying that the air of every place is agreeable to men except the wind of evil passions!'" (ii. 541).

In the end the Emperor permitted Azam to come to Court, and he arrived there on 25th March, 1706. (*M.A.* 512).

### C. Kam Bakhsh.

## § 25. Kam Bakhsh placed under arrest.

The Emperor learnt from the letters of the *nazir* and news-writer with Prince Muhammad Kam Bakhsh,—"After the capture of fort Jinji, Nusrat Jang Khan made a request to the prince to march and halt cautiously as there were more than 50,000 cavalry of the enemy around [the Mughal force]. The prince displaying roughness answered, 'I am my own master. I shall march whenever I like'—till at last the matter passed into unpleasantness. The Khan gave up waiting on the prince in his Court, and interviewed him [only] when riding out. On Wednesday, the 9th Ziqada [=13th July, 1692] at noon when the prince had dismounted in his own camp, he sent a slave to call the Khan, and the latter delayed coming. Four slaves came in quick succession. At this juncture the Khan's spies brought him news that the prince had formed a plan with his foster-brother to imprison the Khan. Also from the letter of the *nazir* it became known that this report was true. The Khan called together the [news]-writers, took them as his witnesses, himself with Rao Dalpat Bundela went riding on elephants to inside the screen *(jali)* [of the prince's quarters], and pulled down the prince's Court-tent with the elephant's trunk. The prince, on seeing this, wanted to flee to his *harem.* But Rao Dalpat coming up seized both his hands, and pulling him by the sleeves dragged him to the elephant of the Khan, who made a sign to Dalpat to seat the prince on his own elephant. So in that manner four marches were made, the prince remaining with Rao Dalpat day and night and staying in his tent."

After reading the sheet, the Emperor wrote on it: (*Verse*)

"A slave-girl's son comes to no good,
Even though he may have been begotten by a king.

What reform could Noah (**on the prophets and on him be peace!**) effect in his disobedient son, that I can succeed [in the same work]? Nusrat Jang Khan is not without wisdom. Whosoever speaks ill of him is himself a bad man. As for bringing this worthless [prince], the leader of the wicked, let Nusrat Jang Khan accompany (*i.e.*, escort) him up to Bijapur, and thereafter entrust him to the prime-minister. Send a *farman* to the governor of Bijapur, to give him an escort of one thousand cavalry and send him to me. Nusrat Jang Khan should go to guard the newly conquered territory, such as fort Jinji and other places. When I send him a *farman*, he will come to me." On the margin of the petition, His Majesty wrote, "For the sake of a son who, agreeably with the verse '**He is your enemy**', has been proved and ascertained to be an enemy,—why should I quarrel with my friends, among whom a good servant is reckoned one? Especially when that servant is a near kinsman, being the son of my maternal aunt, and regard for the friendliness due to kindred is proper." [MS. N. adds,—On the margin he wrote, "Plato has said, '**Your friends are three: the sharer of your salt** (*e. i.*, **meals), the sharer of your danger and the companion of your travels.**' "]

*Text.*—Ir. MS. *22a* & *b*, MS. N. *27b*—*29a*.

*Notes.*—Kam Bakhsh, the youngest and petted son of Aurangzib and Udaipuri Mahal, (born 24 February, 1667) joined the siege of Jinji on 16th Dec., 1691, the real commanders being Asad Khan and his son Nusrat Jang. The fort fell on 7th January, 1698. But about 28th Dec. 1692 Kam Bakhsh, for his opposition to the two generals and intrigue with the enemy, was arrested and sent to the Court, where he arrived on 14th June, 1693 (*M. A.* 355-359). See *History of Aurangzib*, vol. v. ch. 51.

D. Bidar Bakht (son of Azam Shah).

## § 26. Bidar Bakht punished for neglect of duty.

The Emperor learnt from the letter of the *nazir* accompanying Bidar Bakht Bahadur that he had at first greatly exerted himself to capture the fort of Sinsani, belonging to Rajaram Jat, and that it became afterwards known that he had sent a verbal message to the latter, which was evidently this that he should give his brother's daughter to the prince and himself go out of the fort.

Across the sheet the Emperor wrote, "There is no harm. Giving a daughter is a mark of submission. He may go out of the fort, but where will he go outside the imperial territory ? But (*verse*)

What sort of man was he who was less than a woman ?
A man submissive to women is worse than a woman.

The bringing up of children belongs to fathers and not to grandfathers. Prince Alijah (Muhammad Azam), out of his negligent nature and affection for Bidar Bakht's late mother, has brought matters to such a pass. To wise men a straitened condition which is [caused by] punishment in money is the greatest calamity and distress. For one year reduce the *jagir* of his rank (*mansab*) by one-half."

*Text.*—Ir. MS. 21*b* & 22*a* : MS. N. 27*a* & *b* differs a good deal, but only verbally.

*Notes.*—Muhammad Bidar Bakht, the son of Prince Muhammad Azam and Jahanzeb Banu Begam (the daughter of Dara), was born 4th August, 1670. All three of them were greatly loved by Aurangzib, and Bidar Bakht was the old Emperor's special favourite. With Khan-i-Jahan he led an expedition against Rajaram Jat, the rebel chief of Sinsani, who was slain on 4th July, 1688, (*M. A.* 311). Sinsani was captured by him in January, 1690 (*M. A.* 334). *History of Aurangzib*, v. 298).

'Late mother' is incorrect, as the lady died long afterwards, in March, 1705. (*M. A.* 494).

## § 27. Quarrel between Bidar Bakht and his wife.

From the letter of the *nazir* accompanying Prince Bidar Bakht Bahadur, the Emperor learnt, "The prince had always before this shown the greatest affection and favour to Shams-un-nisa, the daughter of Mukhtar Khan. But now, contrary to his usual manner, he often treats her with displeasure, so that one day he had said, 'The daughter of a rascal (*paji*) ought not to show such pride to princes.' At this Shams-un-nisa replied, 'If you like you may slay me, but I shall not speak to you again.' So from that day she had given up speaking to him."

Across the sheet of the letter the Emperor wrote ; (*Verse*)

"At dawn the bird of the garden [ nightingale ]
said to the newly blossomed rose,
'Don't give yourself airs so much, because in this
garden many like you had budded [before.]'
The rose laughed [saying], 'I am not
sorry to hear the truth, but
No lover ever spoke a bitter word to his beloved.'

(*Hafiz*)

Be it clear to this light of my eye [*i.e.*, grandson] that in the season of youth, which in the vile phraseology of his boon companions is styled 'mad youth,' I, too, had this relation with a person [wife] who had extreme imperiousness, but to the end of her life I continued to love her and never once did I wound her feelings. Then, again, to apply the term *paji* to Sayyids is simply to act like a *paji*. If a Sayyid is called a *paji*, it will not certainly make her a *paji*. If I do not learn from the letters of the *mahaldar* and the *nazir* that you have made it up with this Sayyid girl, you will meet with rebuke, nay more, with punishment. **[God shall give them] recompense for that which they were doing.**"

*Text.*—MS. N. 23*b* 1—24*a* 5.

*Notes.*—Bidar Bakht, the son of Azam, and the favourite grandson of Aurangzib, was married to the daughter of Mukhtar Khan, surnamed Puti Begam, on 21st Nov., 1686 (*M. A.* 284). A son, named Firuz Bakht was born to them on 23rd Aug., 1695 (*Ibid.* 374), Bidar Bakht's father-in-law was Qamr-ud-din, the son of Shams-ud-din, the son of Sayyid Muhammad, all three of them being successively entitled Mukhtar Khan (*M. U.* iii. 656). This family, the Ben-i-Mukhtar, enjoyed the greatest respect among the Muslims, and traced its descent from the Prophet, through Abul Mukhtar, the *naqib* of Ali's Mashhad and *Amir-ul-haj*. One of its members migrated from Najaf to Sabzawar in Khurasan, hence their title of Sabzawari. (*M. U.* iii. 409).

Aurangzib is referring to his own married life. His wife Dilras Banu, the daughter of Shah Nawaz Khan Safawi, (married 8th May, 1637, d. 8 October, 1657), must have been a very proud woman, if we can judge her character from that of her son, Muhammad Azam, who was incredibly vain and haughty.

## SECTION III.

## ABOUT HIS OFFICERS

### § 28. Humiliation of Nusrat Jang.

WHEN Zulfiqar Khan Bahadur Nusrat Jang, after the capture of Jinji, arrived within 4 *koses** of the imperial camp at Panhala, Sarbarah Khan, the *kotwal*, reported to the Emperor that an imperial order had been issued [to Nusrat Jang] for the chastisement of the enemy [*i.e.*, the Marathas] roving in the direction of the Base Camp, and [yet] the Khan had arrived near the imperial camp. The Emperor said, "Don't give him a pass to enter the lines of the army. Yar Ali Beg, who is the [Court] agent of Nusrat Jang, should write about this matter to him." Next morning he entered the imperial encampment without a pass and demanded permission for admission to the Emperor's private audience. His Majesty ordered that Nusrat Jang should come to the presence with his quiver and pouch [of ammunition] fastened to his waist, his bow on his shoulders, and his musket in his hand, and that, contrary to the former practice, when his *palki* used to come up to the network-fence (*jali*) of the Private Audience Hall, he should that day leave his *palki* inside the network-fence near the two *rawtis* (small square tents) of the Hall of Private Audience. Yar Ali Beg wrote [to Nusrat Jang] all about these ironical favours due to anger. The Khan dismounted at the *gulal-bar* (red canvas wall forming the outermost limit of the Emperor's own quarters), stripped

---

* MS. N. reads *fourteen koses*.

off all weapons from his person, and walking on foot towards the presence chamber, sat down in the *rawti* at the door of the Private Audience Hall, waiting for an order for his presentation. He passed two *gharis* in silence and neglect, and was then permitted to enter. As he wished to kiss the Emperor's toes, His Majesty extended his right leg. On account of his great confusion and agitation, Nusrat Jang's knees touched the cushion (*masnad*) of the Emperor, who was displeased at it, but with extreme kindness and favour laid his hand on the Khan's back and said, "You were absent for a long time and so have forgotten the etiquette of the Court. (*Verse*).

A crow turned its tail to the city and its head to the village;
[Surely] the crow's tail was better than its head !"

Then the Emperor turned his face towards Bahramand Khan and said, "How can it be that servants brought up in my household would unlearn etiquette by reason of their going away from the Court? Evidently this Khan's eyesight has been affected." So he ordered Muharram Khan to bring a pair of spectacles and with his own hands place them on Nusrat Jang's nose, and also insisted that he should go to his quarters in that guise, and that as it was a gift from the Emperor he should for three days come to the *darbar* wearing the spectacles, as was the rule when robes of honour were presented.

When Nusrat Jang saw this disgrace, he, through the intercession of Amir Khan, the superintendent (*darogha*) of the Emperor's personal servants (*khawas*), at night secured permission to depart for the punishment of the Marathas. After the *'isha* prayer he came with the spectacles on, had audience in the room where the Emperor counted his beads, and took his leave.

*Text.*—Irvine MS. 1*b*—2*a*. MS. N. 37*b*—39*a*.

*Notes.*—Zulfiqar Khan, surnamed Nusrat Jang Bahadur, was a son of Aurangzib's prime-minister Asad Khan. (Born 1657 A. D., executed in 1713). The fort of Jinji (or Gingee in the South Arcot District) capitulated to him on 7th January, 1698. Panhala was besieged by Aurangzib from 9th March to 28th May, 1701. The Base Camp was at Islampuri on the Bhima river. Bahramand Khan was the chief paymaster, (died 5th November, 1702). Amir Khan was Mir Abdul Karim (son of Amir Khan Shah Jahani). A *ghari* is 24 minutes.

## § 29. **Obey orders first.**

Zulfiqar Khan Bahadur Nusrat Jang had by order gone in pursuit of Hanumant [Rao Nimbalkar], the infidel commander [of the Marathas]. By chance he passed within four miles of the imperial encampment. So, he petitioned, "As it has happened by chance that I have to pass close to the Emperor's army, I consider it a breach of etiquette to go away without waiting upon your Majesty." On the application the Emperor wrote, "Two things have been done by you contrary to good manners: first, why have you let the brigands pass close to the imperial encampment? This act was not free from bad manners, nay, it was likely to prove a fault on your part. Secondly, by not engaging in the work entrusted to you and by making a request contrary to it, you have shown disobedience. **Obey God, obey the Prophet, and obey the commanders (kings) among you!"**

*Text.*—Ir. MS. 21*a* & *b*.

## § 30. Presumptuousness of a Deccani officer.

From the news-letter of the army of Zulfiqar Khan Nusrat Jang, the Emperor learnt that Jang-ju Khan Deccani, who held the rank of a Commander of Five Thousand cavalry, had placed his kettledrums on buffaloes and in a mischievous spirit had ordered them to be carried side by side with the kettledrums of the band of Nusrat Jang on an equal footing. The Emperor wrote, "What harm does it do to me, and what objection has Nusrat Jang Khan to it? So long as this chief of the accursed and disgraced tribe does not understand his own parading (*tashhir*), which is the height of disgrace, even if he were to carry his drums in advance of those of Nusrat Jang, it would be just what [we] desire! His marching abreast of Nusrat Jang, too, is no small disgrace to him."

*Text.*—Ir. MS. 3*b*—4*a*, not in MS. N.

*Notes.*—*Tashhir* is a mode of punishment in which a man is publicly disgraced by being paraded through a city or camp mounted on an ass and accompanied by noisy music, in parody of a royal procession. (*Mughal Administration*. 2nd ed., p. 121.)

## § 31. Faithlessness of Deccani officers.

The news-reporter of Nusrat Jang wrote to the Emperor that Zindan Khan Deccani, who held the rank of a Commander of Four Thousand in the muster-roll (*zabita*) of the Deccan, used to sacrifice his life in the service of the Emperor, and hence it would be proper to confer a higher rank on him. Nusrat Jang Khan, too, wrote to the Emperor to the same effect. The Emperor wrote this order;—"The term 'sacrificing his life' is a mere piece of rhetoric and a fashion of speech. If he repeatedly sacrificed his life, how is it possible for him to be still alive? To show favour to this race (*i.e.*, the Deccanis) is to take up a scorpion by the hand or keep a serpent in the arms. **The people of Kufa are faithless.**"

*Text.*—Ir. MS. 4*a*, not in MS. N.

*Notes.*—This contempt for Deccani officers was unjust. It was a Deccani officer who, by great activity, courage and enterprise, captured Shambhuji. Kufa is a town, west of the Euphrates and east of Mashhad, the inhabitants of which proved false to Husain and thus lured him to his death at Karbala.

## § 32. Beware of the Sayyids of Barha!

From the report of the province of Nander the Emperor learnt that Sayyid Hasan Ali Khan Bahadur had shown great activity in fighting with Hanumant, the general of the misbelievers [Marathas], sacked his base-camp (*bungah*), taken alive the brother's son of Janaji and imposed on him the honour of conversion to Islam. Zulfiqar Khan Bahadur Nusrat Jang, who was passing by that place for chastising the disturber Dhana Jadav, recommended promotions for both the [Sayyid] brothers and sent the letter of recommendation to the Emperor by relays of couriers (*dak*), praying that the elder brother's rank, which was 800, might be raised to 1000, and the younger brother's, which was 700, to 900.

Across the sheet [of the report] the Emperor wrote, "Bravo! Why should it not be so? The Sayyids, who are sources of auspiciousness, bear this meaning that they should try with all their life for supporting the strong faith of their forefather, His Holiness the Sayyid among prophets [Muhammad]. Send to both the brothers with [a mace-bearer] two robes of honour from the royal wardrobe, with two daggers set with plain-work jasper and having pearl straps. The prime-minister should write a 'Letter By Order' full of praise and send it to them."

Across the letter [of Nusrat Jang] His Majesty wrote, "The recommendation of promotion made by this hereditary servant aware of my sentiments, was very proper. Failure on the part of generals to conciliate good soldiers is a matter of regret. It should not be done. But it is difficult [for me] to consent to their promotion in one step. True, love for the high-ranked Sayyids is a part of our faith, nay more, it is the very essence of spiritual knowledge; and enmity to this tribe is the cause of entry into hell-fire and of [incurring] the anger of God. But we should not do an act which might be a source of our grief in this world and misery in the next. To relax the reins to the Sayyids of Barha is to bring on final ruin, *i. e.*, a bad end; because these people on getting the least prosperity and promotion boast, 'There is none like me', stray from the path of right conduct, cherish high views, and cause impediment. If [then] they are neglected, worldly affairs become difficult to perform. If they are corrected, the feet ultimately fall into mud."

*Text.*—Ir. MS. 26*b* & 27*a*.

*Notes.*—Sayyid Hasan Ali Khan of Barha afterwards became Qutb-ul-mulk Abdullah Khan and the *wazir* of Farrukhsiyar. He is known to fame as one of the "Sayyid Brothers" or Indian King-makers. In Aurangzib's reign he was faujdar of Nandurbar and Sultanpur. (Life in *M. U.* iii. 130-140). Hasan Ali's heroic but disastrous fight with the Marathas under Nima Sindhia (1698) is described by Khafi Khan, ii. 457. His brother Husain Ali Khan, afterwards created Amir-ul-umara, became faujdar of Hindun-Biana under Aurangzib. (Life in *M. U.* i. 321—338). Their father Sayyid Abdullah was appointed faujdar of Nander in Feb. 1690, (*M. A.* 335) and is spoken of as subahdar of it in 1695 (*Akh.*). Nusrat Jang "returned to Court after punishing Dhana Jadav" about January, 1700 (*M. A.* 432). But he had a roving commission from 1701 to 1705 to chastise the Maratha bands wherever found.

## § 33. The Rise of the Nizam's father.

When Ghazi-ud-din Khan Bahadur Firuz Jang, whose original name was Mir Shihab-ud-din, first came to India from *Vilayet*, his father Abid Khan, through the mediation of Sarbuland Khan the Paymaster, introduced him to the Emperor at Delhi in the course of his Majesty's ride on a pilgrimage to the saint Qutb [Shah's tomb], and got for him the rank of a Commander of Three Hundred Horse. Afterwards when the Emperor went to Ajmir, none of the scouts consented [to go out] to bring news about Prince Muhammad Akbar who had gone over to the Rajputs. Mir Shihab-ud-din said, "This slave is willing." The Emperor gave him a robe of honour and a promotion of two hundred, and so sent him. On the 14th day the news of his return reached the sentinels round the imperial army, and he too sent a letter saying "This slave has arrived with true news. Please quickly issue an order for my admission into the camp that I may tell it." On the petition the Emperor wrote, (*Verse*)

"Whosoever drinks, like the ruby, the blood of the liver and grows patient,
Becomes the ornament of the top of the crown of Fortune.

The *kotwal* must give him a pass to enter the camp."

*Text.*—Ir. MS. 10*b*, MS. N. 31*b* and 32*a*.

*Notes.*—Mir Shihab-ud-din, surnamed Ghazi-ud-din Khan Firuz Jang, was the son of Abid Khan, *Sadar* of Aurangzib's reign, and the father of the 1st Nizam-ul-mulk (Mir Qamr-ud-din, Chin Qalich Khan, Asaf Jah). Shihabuddin came from his home in Samarqand to seek his fortune at the Court of Delhi in October, 1669. The incident of the present anecdote is also narrated in the *Masir-i-Alamgiri*, p. 185, Khafi Khan, ii. 267, and in his life in the *Masir-ul-umara*, ii. 832 *et seq.* It took place some time *before* Akbar's rebellion. *Vilayet* means any country across the N. W. frontier of India, especially Central Asia. Prince Akbar rebelled against his father in January, 1681. (*Hist. of Aurangzib*, iii. ch. 36.)

## § 34. Trials to be held strictly according to Quranic Law

The Emperor learnt from the news-letter of the army of Firuz Jang Khan that he had, while holding audience, executed a man named Muhammad Aqil on the charge of highway robbery. The Emperor wrote, "The prime-minister [Asad Khan] should write thus to the foolish Khan Firuz Jang,—you have undertaken an execution, *i.e.*, the destruction of what God had built, without proof according to Canon Law. Alas for the day when the heirs of [the slain] will arrive and refuse to accept the price of his blood! How can this humble being [Aurangzib] help giving the order of retaliation [on you], as mercy in the exercise of penal laws (*hadud*) is contrary to the authority of the Word of God [*i.e.*, the Quran]? **And kindness should not overpower you in [matters concerning] the religion of God.**"

*Text.*—Ir. MS. 3*b*, MS. N. 9*a*.

*Notes.*—Ghazi-ud-din Khan Firuz Jang Bahadur, the father of the first Nizam of Haidarabad, was one of the two highest generals of Aurangzib, the other being his rival Nusrat Jang. (Died 1710 A. D.) *The price of blood* is the money-compensation for which the heirs of a murdered man may, under the Islamic law, give up their demand for the execution of the murderer. For this term and *hadud*, see my *Mughal Administration*, 2nd ed. ch. 6.

## § 35. Preaches meekness to Firuz Jang.

The Emperor learnt from the news-letter of Ghazi-ud-din Khan Bahadur Firuz Jang, that the Khan had laid it down that in the orders which he sent to various places the phrase 'By the *karamat-buniad* command [of the Khan]' should be written.

The Emperor wrote, "No harm. His ancestors were hermits and inmates of monasteries. I allow the use of 'By command' only. But a Commander of Seven Thousand does not possess miraculous power (*karamat*). I order that in future the customary present on the Emperor's coronation anniversary which he will send to [us] his slaves, will not be accepted [by us]."

When Ghazi-ud-din Khan got news of it, he petitioned thus, **"He who repents of a sin becomes sinless as it were, and when a man confesses a fault verily God forgives all his faults, few and many."** On the petition the Emperor wrote, **"Whosoever earns the pardon of his affliction by means of reformation, God will recompense him. And if a man returns to his sins, God wreaks vengeance on him."**

*Text.*—Ir. MS. 24*b* & 25*a*.

*Notes.*—Ghazi-ud-din Khan, the father of the first Nizam-ul-mulk, was the grandson of Alam Shaikh, a scholar and saint of Samarqand, (*M. U.* iii. 837, 120), who claimed descent from Shaikh Shihab-ud-din Saharawardi, a renowned saint of Central Asia. There is a play upon the phrase *karamat-buniad*, which may mean (1) gracious and (2) miracle-working. Aurangzib takes it in the latter sense, hence his objection and ironical remark that he is only a slave of Firuz Jang.

## § 36. Kindness to Hamid Khan Bahadur.

The Emperor learnt from the news-letter of the army of Hamid Khan Bahadur, the brother of Ghazi-ud-din Khan Firuz Jang, that though not granted this distinction by the Emperor, he carried with himself kettledrums and bandsmen, and every day played the *naubat* as at festivities. On the sheet the Emperor wrote, "The brother of Firuz Jang Khan is not such a fool as to act so very audaciously. It is evident that there is some festival [or other] in his house everyday. As even low persons do not require permission from the Emperor to play the *naubat* on festive occasions, why should he? In future the news-writer must not spitefully bring such charges against him. I admire his patience that while, in spite of his holding the rank of a Commander of Four Thousand horse and the title *Bahadur*, I have not granted him the right to play the *naubat* in view of the littleness of his wisdom, he himself has not once asked [for this mark of distinction]."

*Text*—Ir. MS. 10*b* & 11*a*. MS. N. 11*b* & 12*a*.

*Notes.*—Khwajah Hamid, the son of Qalich Khan (Khwajah Abid) and brother of Firuz Jang, was created Hamid Khan Bahadur in September, 1685; afterwards got the titles of Muiz-ud-daula and Salabat Jang. (Life in *Masir-ul-umara*, iii. 765). In Aurangzib's reign he did not rise to a higher rank than the command of 2500. He was quite distinct from Hamid-*ud-din* Khan Bahadur. Died at Kulbarga, 1140 A.H.

## § 37. Oppressive Governor rebuked.

Khan-i-Jahan Bahadur, who was governor of Lahor, greatly oppressed the inhabitants of the place at the time of his return, so that the matter reached the Emperor's knowledge from the news-reports (*sawanih*). On the day of interview the Emperor told him, "I had not expected this of you. The worst of all [your acts] is that you have set on foot certain innovations (*bidat*, illegal practices) in the *jagirs* appertaining to Lahor which will last for ever. (*Verse*)

Even after his death the tyrant does not cease to oppress.
The plumes of the (dead) eagle become in the end the feathers of arrows!"

*Text.*—Ir. MS. 6*a* & *b*.

*Notes.*—Mir Malik Husain, Bahadur Khan, brother of Azam Khan Kokah, (created Khan-i-Jahan Bahadur Kokaltash in 1673, and Zafar Jang in 1675) was one of the highest officers of Aurangzib and long served in the Deccan. Appointed subahdar of the Panjab, 11th April, 1691 ; but dismissed in the middle of 1693. Died 23rd November, 1697; buried at Nakudar in the Panjab Doab. (Life in *Masir-ul-umara*, i. 798—813).

## § 38. Qualifications of a Governor.

Khwajah Sarbuland Khan, the chief paymaster, whose father belonged to an eminent Khwajah family of Bukhara, was treated with great consideration by the Emperor. Once when His Majesty complained about him, it was only this that his words savoured a little of Shia-ism. He replied, "Ay! your Majesty, in Bukhara many of the Sayyids of Bukhara belong to that sect. Traces of their society have been left [in my speech]. But I have not yet been confirmed in that faith. Through ill luck I have withdrawn myself from this and yet not arrived at that [creed]." The Emperor smiled and gave no reply.

For this reason Sarbuland Khan showed great favour to the Persians and exerted himself much in furthering their affairs, so that he recommended a certain [Persian] lord for the governorship of Kabul. Across the sheet of his petition the Emperor wrote, "I grant the request of this trustworthy servant. Let a robe of honour consisting of six pieces of cloth from my wardrobe be given [to his nominee]. Jewels, horse, and elephant will be presented to him according to the regulations. But remember that this man will not be able to discharge the duties of that post. May God make it end well!"

*Notes.*—Sarbuland Khan, appointed 2nd paymaster in October, 1672 and died in office, 27 December, 1679. (Life in *Masir-ul-umara*, ii. 477). Sarbuland's mother was Ai Begam, a daughter of Mirza Shahrukh, king of Badakhshan.

*Text.*—Ir. MS. 12*b* and MS. R. 15. But in MS. N. 18*a*—20*a*, which also differs a little textually from the Ir. MS., the above order of the Emperor is continued in the following words:—

"—so that it may not be a cause of disgrace and ridicule, and may not make people talk about it for years. This man's thoughts are full of violence and his notion about himself is marked by great confidence and pride. Plato wrote to Alexander, 'Government should be strict without being oppressive, and gentle without being weak.' This noble has extreme severity and obstinate adhesion to one policy only, inasmuch as he has never known subterfuge. Besides, he is very honest and simple-minded, as he cannot at all understand fraud and stratagem. One cannot rule without practising deception. The clear text of the Holy Traditions [of Muhammad] is **'War is stratagem.'** The science of Jurisprudence has many component parts. It is most likely that the art of government is included in this total. In the days when I was going to take up the governorship of the Deccan, I met at Burhanpur a *darvish* who was a master of *taksir* (word-breaking and word-forming). He had learnt some examples of this art from his preceptor, and he also now and then composed some others himself. It is a fixed rule of *taksir* that if we strike off the common letters from the two lines of *taksir*, we can extract a meaning from the words [which may be formed from the remaining letters] consistently with sense. So that, if the words *hakumat* (government) and *hilat* (cunning) are arranged in two lines, and the common letters are cancelled, the words *kul*, *yum*, and *malik* are derived [from the remainder] by combination (*qalb*), and we get **malik-i-kul-yum** * (king for all time), that is to say, a government that is joined to cunning lasts and remains firm for ever and the master of this [art of government] becomes 'a king for all time.'

In the opinion of the common herd, cunning and deception are greatly scorned. As God himself in His Holy Word [*i., e.*, the Quran] has ascribed cunning to His own holy self, saying, '**God is the best of plotters**,'†

---

* It is done in the following manner:

H K U M T (*hakumat*)
H Y L T (*hilat*)

Cancelling the common letters H and T, we can form, by combinations of the remaining 5 letters, only these words 'bearing a sense,' *viz.*, *kul*, *yum*, and *malik*. Thus is proved the precious doctrine that if a ruler combines *hakumat* and *hilat* he becomes *malik-i-kul-yum* !!!

† That is, God's ways are inscrutable to men and He sometimes seems to deceive mortals in His dealings with them. *Cf.* Milton's *Samson Agonistes*, ll. 350—360, 667—686.

it is contrary to the Quran to consider stratagem as blamable. Besides, in governing Kabul this quality is most beneficial and excellent. (*Verse*)

I am speaking to you what is required by eloquence ;
You take wisdom from it or feel displeased, [as you like]."

*Text.*—MS. N. 19*a* 2—20*a* 5.

## § 39. Ability the only qualification for office.

Muhammad Amin Khan, on his first arrival in India from *Vilayet*, was created a Commander of Five Hundred, in consideration of the fact that his father had been faithful to Prince Alamgir during the war in Balkh and had rendered good service. In the course of time he received praise, was repeatedly promoted, and attained to the rank of a Commander of Three Thousand (two thousand additional troopers) and the distinction of playing *naubat*, for his activity against the accursed enemy [the Marathas], bringing forage (*khai*) from Satara and other places, convoying provisions, and going to and from every [Mughal] entrenchment. As the Emperor wished that the Khan should remain away [from the imperial encampment] for some time and play the *naubat*, he said, "I learn from the news reports that the revenue coming from Bengal has crossed the Narmada. You should go and halt at Aurangabad, in order that you may at last enjoy some respite from movement, and play the *naubat* granted to you to your heart's content." Then His Majesty dismissed him, after presenting him with the riding cloak trimmed with fur and richly laced which he was himself wearing.

When the Khan returned with the revenue, after fighting with the shameless Marathas, gaining victories, and convoying the Government treasure in safety, His Majesty presented him with a horse adorned with gold trappings, a dagger with a *kalgi*, and the robe of honour worn on his august person. When he saw these successive favours, he submitted a petition through Muharram Khan, saying, "In view of the obedience and old service which the aged slave had performed in Balkh, this devoted servant had hoped for favours ; but owing to the large number of his enemies and the fewness of his friends [at Court] he had not so long made bold to submit his wishes. [But now] relying on God he makes this petition."

*Copy of the petition*: "Hail ! saint and spiritual guide of the world and of its people ! Both the paymasterships have been conferred on heretical demon-natured Persians. If one of the paymasterships be given to this old and devoted servant, it would be a means of strengthening the [Sunni] faith and of snatching away employment from accursed misbelievers. **O, ye faithful ! do not take as friends your own and our enemies.**"

Across the sheet of the petition Aurangzib wrote, "What you have stated about your long service is true. It is being appreciated as far as possible. As for what you have written about the false creed of the Persians, [I answer],—'What connection have worldly affairs with religion ? and what right have matters of religion to enter into bigotry ? **For you is your religion and for me is mine.**' If this rule [suggested by you] were established, it would be my duty to extirpate all the (Hindu) Rajahs and their followers. Wise men disapprove of the removal from office of able officers. Your request for a paymastership is appropriate, as you hold a rank suited to the post. The reason that acts as a hindrance is that the Turani people, your followers, who are clansmen from the same city as that of my ancestors,—according to the saying '**Don't throw yourself into destruction with your own hands,**'—do not think it a shame to retreat in the very thick of the battle. It would not be a great harm if this sort of thing took place in a foraging expedition, but it would cause a terrible difficulty if it occurred in the midst of a [regular] battle. If, **God forbid it!** the attendants of the Emperor were to act thus, then in a moment all would be over [with him].

If you have [ever] declined this actually experienced and tested business (*viz.* retreat), write to me in detail [about it]. The Persians, whether born in *Vilayet* or in Hindustan—who (the last) are noted for their gross stupidity,—are a hundred stages removed from this sort of movement [*i.e.*, flight.] (*Verse*)

> Do justice, as the folly of these bad men
> Is better than a thousand brains of the fox-natured.
> One brain is enough for an army
> For throwing bricks from engines into the eyes of the enemy."

*Text.*—Ir. MS. 14*a*—15*a*.

*Notes.*—Muhammad Amin Khan, the son of Mir Baha-ud-din, who was the brother of Qalich Khan, came to India from Bukhara in 1687 ; got the title of *Chin Bahadur* (Nov. 1706) and the post of *Sadar* (1698). At the time of Aurangzib's death he was a Commander of 4000, (1500 additional troopers). For his attachment to his Mughal followers, see *Masir-ul-umara*, i. 349.

## § 40. Aurangzib preaches humility to an officer.

Yar Ali Beg submitted to the Emperor, on the basis of an oral report from a spy, that while Hamid-ud-din Khan Bahadur was bandying words with Muhammad Murad *qul*, the latter said 'You little man (*mardak*)! you are a *chela*, (slave) of the Emperor just as I am'; and that at this Hamid-ud-din Khan resigned his post and sent the letter of resignation to Bahramand Khan, the chief paymaster. The Emperor wrote, "The word *mardak* was not employed in abuse; it is a diminutive, meaning 'a little man.' The men of the world are not at all great men. Probably the Khan Bahadur felt ashamed at being called *chela*. (*Verse*)

Whosoever quarrels with a man lower than himself,
Tears up his own *parda* (honour) sooner than the latter's.
Every wise man who enters into a dispute with a worthless man,
Only strikes his own lustrous jewel (*i. e.*, intellect or character) on a hard stone."

*Text.*—Ir. MS. 16*a* & *b*.

*Notes.*—Hamid-ud-din Khan Bahadur, surnamed *Nimchah-i-Alamgirshahi*, was the son of Ihtamam Khan (Sardar Khan), and greatly distinguished himself by his fights with the Marathas. (Life in *Masir-ul-umara*, i. 605—611). *Qul* is a Turkish word meaning a slave. The Emperor Akbar changed the title of the imperial slaves from *ghulam* (slave) to *chela* (disciple), because he considered it an act of impious presumptuousness for one mortal to call another his *ghulam*, all men being the *ghulams* of God only. (Masum's *Tarikh-i-Shujai*, 143*a*; *Ain*. i. 253).

## § 41. Proverty is no hindrance where there is a will.

In the 32nd year of Aurangzib's reign, Mirza Sadr-ud-din Muhammad Khan Safawi, (who was ultimately given the title of Shah Nawaz Khan), was dismissed from his rank for making an improper request. The Emperor settled on him an annual stipend of Rs. 40,000. After a year His Majesty recollected the claims of his father, Mirza Sultan Safawi, who had shown great constancy during the war with Dara Shukoh. So, he sent a gracious *farman* summoning him to Court with a special robe of honour, by the hand of mace-bearers. The Khan after taking the *farman* kissed it, put on the robe, and after showing the proper etiquette sent a petition, to say, "Owing to the poverty resulting from my long deprivation of rank, I am not able to engage a body of retainers with whom I may attend Court. So, I am waiting for the *caravan* from Bengal [to escort me]." The Emperor wrote, (*verse*)

"The odour of the rose and the morning breeze are out on the road,
If you wish to go out of yourself, there is no beter caravan than these.
Alas that the objects that captivate the heart
Are as close together as the links of a chain!

Outwardly your excuse is reasonable, but in fact the weakness of your spirit [is the cause of your] straitened means. O, God! show the path to all whose steps are weak!"

*Text.*—Ir. MS. 16*b*.

*Notes.*—Mirza Sultan (*M. U.* iii. 581) was devoted to Aurangzib during the war of succession, but did not fight, as he was left behind at Aurangabad. His son, Sadr-ud-din, rose to be paymaster under Aurangzib and was created Shah Nawaz Khan by Bahadur Shah I. (Life in *M. U.* iii. 692).

## § 42. A silent suppliant.

The Emperor told Bahramand Khan, who was paymaster at that time, "Musavi Khan *alias* Mirza Muizz-i-Fitrat, out of pride never petitions me about his wants and is living in great distress. Unless he writes to me about his circumstances, he will get no favour from me. You should send him word [about it], get in reply a petition from him, and submit it to me." So, after receiving the message, Musavi Khan wrote to the Emperor, **"Your knowledge of my condition is better than my words.** (*Verse*)

In demanding, we speechless ones belong to the race of moths :
To me it is easier to burn [in the fire of desire] than to state my wish.
My tongue of statement has become silent from my pride of service.
These meritorious deeds have thrown me into the path of mistake.
The ocean of mercy never reposes from [heaving in] billows of gracious acts.
(Hence) those who beg make needless importunity."

The Emperor wrote on the petition, "Verily you have written the truth. (*Verse*)

Silence opens the hardest prisons.
In the cage the parrot with its beak is [vainly] chattering about itself.

But,

No man is engaged in mending his own character;
Every one whom I have seen is busy in pampering his own nature (passions).

According to the Tradition, **'The king is the shadow of God,'** whenever the king of the age requests his servant to state his desires, and the latter gives such an excellent answer, it would be bad manners not to grant favours to him."

*Text.*—Ir. MS. 18*b*.

*Notes.*—Mirza Muizz, a Persian of Mashhad, married a sister of Aurangzib's wife and was created Musavi Khan and *diwan* of the Pay office (*daftar-i-tan*) in September, 1688, and *diwan* of the Deccan in June, 1689. Died after May, 1690. (*Masir-i-Alamgiri*, 337 and 338. Life in *M. U.* iii. 633). His poetical pseudonyms were *Fitrat* and *Musavi*. In Persian poetry the moth which silently burns itself in the flame is the emblem of the highest kind of lovers.

## § 43. Work for your wages.

Mukhlis Khan petitioned the Emperor to grant an increment, half in cash salary and half in *jagir*, to Sultan Mahmud, one of the pure-born Sayyids of the holy city of Mashhad, who was living in a very distressed condition, and whom the Khan greatly supported.

The Emperor wrote on the petition:—"**The good deeds we do are for our own benefit, the sins we commit shall lie on ourselves.** I know full well the saintliness and piety of that Sayyid. But he is not attached to any post. A hired labourer should not consider his wages as lawfully earned unless he has done some service,—which is a good and virtuous deed. (*Verse*)

Although you cannot untie a knot with your toes,
The knots of livelihood are opened by the exertions of
the feet (*i.e.*, active service)."

*Text.*—Ir. MS. 6*b*.

## § 44. Charity covers a multitude of sins.

From the news-letter of the office (*kachari*) of the High Diwan the Emperor learnt that Mir Habibullah of Jaunpur, the *amin* of the poll-tax on non-Muslims (*jaziya*), had misappropriated beyond a doubt Rs. 40,000 from the imperial charity treasury (*bait-ul-mal*), and that he had also admitted it. Inayetullah Khan had placed him under detention in the office and appointed strict *sazawals* (collectors) to exact the money from him. The aforesaid Sayyid was saying, "I have only a life, but no earthly property in my possession."

Across the sheet of the news-letter the Emperor wrote, "Why do you try to realize again money which has been already recovered by me ? From the reports of Burhanpur I had repeatedly learnt before this that the aforesaid Sayyid was spending all his earnings on deserving mendicants and in works of charity. As the money of this sinner sunk in sin (*i.e.*, Aurangzib) has been spent by means of this my agent in deeds of charity, its restitution is unprofitable. **God save us from the wickedness of our passions !"**

*Text.*—Ir. MS. 17*a*.

## § 45. The mystic number Twelve.

When the Emperor marched from Islampuri (otherwise called Brahmapuri) in the month of Jamadi-us-sani of the 42nd year of his reign, to conquer the forts of the Deccan,—he ordered that every day Mukhlis Khan, the second paymaster, should present to His Majesty ten mansabdars (military officers) from among the hereditary servants (*khanahzad*) and others, but excluding the Deccanis. The Khan submitted, "As your Majesty has followed the verse **'These are the ten perfect ones,'** in ordering that ten officers with their retinue (*misl*) should be daily paraded before you, it is good. Otherwise, if the number be twelve, there is no harm." The Emperor replied, "Your request, too, is not unsupported by [scriptural] authority. (*Verse*)

Behold the hours of the day and the Signs of the Zodiac,
Day and night and the heavens too obey the number twelve!"

Muhammad Amin Khan said, "Ay, companionship has a wonderful effect, as I find to-day. Why should there not be four instead of twelve?" His Majesty replied, "Four is included in twelve." He smiled and continued, "Why is it not three, [you might ask]. But twelve is related to three as the double of double. You are free to choose. Do whatever is likely to benefit the creatures of God most."

*Text.*—Ir. MS. 16*b* & 17*a*.

*Notes.*—Aurangzib marched out of Islampuri, on 5th Jamadi-ul-awwal, in the 43rd year of his reign (=19 October, 1699) to conquer the Maratha forts. Mukhlis Khan, appointed 2nd pay-master in July, 1692, died 3 January, 1701. Muhammad Amin Khan Chin Bahadur was Sadar at this time. One section of the Shias are *followers of the twelve* [ Imams ].

## § 46. Kings should never rest.

After the conquest of Bijapur and Haidarabad, the prime-minister petitioned the Emperor, "Praised be God! that through the grace of the Great Omnipotent and the never-to-decay fortune [of your Majesty], two great kingdoms have been conquered. It is now good policy that the imperial standards should return to Paradise-like Hindustan (*i.e.*, Northern India), so that the world may know that nothing more remains for the Emperor to do [here]."

The Emperor wrote [across the letter], "I wonder how an all-knowing hereditary servant like you could make such a request. If your wish is that men might know that no work now remains to be done, it would be contrary to truth. So long as a single breath of this mortal life remains, there is no release from labour and work. (*Verse*)

The traveller in the path of long hopes needs no guide.
So long as a breath remains, the path of life is not smooth.
It is hard that my runaway heart longs for home,
The dew has so passed away and yet it still remembers the garden.

If Shah Jahan had not chosen to stay at Delhi and Agra, but had been constantly out on tour, his affairs would not have come to the pass that they actually did. If out of regard for good manners you do not [again] make such a request, and can bear the hardships of the expeditions for capturing forts,—then in future I shall turn to the siege of forts. (*Verse*)

What fear of danger has the man drowned in love?
What anxiety about headache has the man who has lost his head?

Praised be God that in whatever place and abode I have been, I have by passing [through it] withdrawn my heart from all things connected with it, and made death easy for myself. (*Verse*)

Untie little by little the knot tying your heart [to earthly things],
Or else, Death will snatch away this string all at once and unawares."

*Text.*—Ir. MS. 17*b* and 18*a*

## § 47. Rigorous marching even in illness.

When the Emperor marched from Brahmapuri, which he had named Islampuri, in order to capture [the Maratha] forts, he ordered that whether he was sick or well there should be no halt on any day except Friday. So that, before reaching Khawaspur where his knee was hurt, he had two severe fits of illness, once fever, and another time diarrhœa; yet except on Friday there was never a halt. During illness he used to be carried in a sedan chair (*takht-i-rawan*) with an open top, whereas in health he rode in a chair with glass [sides]. By chance, it was on a Thursday night that his knee got hurt at Khawaspur. Immediately he said, "Strike the kettledrums for a march." Hamid-ud-din Khan, by reason of his being very bold, submitted, "It would be contrary to what you had fixed when leaving Islampuri." His Majesty smiled and said, "If you had the least knowledge of the science of logic, you would not have said so. I was then referring to the question of halting or not on days other than Friday. My object was to arrange for the march, and not that there must be a halt on every Friday. An opposite conception does not conflict with the validity of the original."

*Text.*—MS. N. 7*b* 2—11 and then 33*a* 1—8.

*Notes.*—Aurangzib set out from Islampuri on 19th October, 1699 (*M. A.* 408), and arrived at Khawaspur on 30th August, 1700 (430). Aurangzib means to say that the expression "there should be a march on all the days of the week other than Friday" does not logically imply that there would be no march on Friday. For the hurt to his leg, see *Hist. of Aurangzib*, v. 171.

## § 48. A profligate noble punished.

Mirza Tafakhkhur, the son of the prime-minister [Asad Khan]'s daughter, acquired ruffianly habits at Delhi, laid the hand of oppression on the property and honour [*i.e.*, women] of the people, often came to the bazar with his comrades, plundered the shops of the grocers, confectioners and others, and with the help of his men seized the Hindu women who went to the river to bathe, and did them all sorts of disgrace and dishonour. Every time that this matter was brought to the Emperor's notice in the news-letters and reports, he wrote "The prime-minister" and nothing more.

At last the Emperor repeatedly learnt that while a *Baksaria* named Ghanashyam, having just married, was passing with his companions by the gate of Mirza Tafakhkhur, placing his wife in a *dooli* and himself on horseback, the ruffians informed the Mirza, who sallied forth with a party of them, and dragged the *dooli* by force into his own house. Two men were killed and six wounded [in the affray]. The men of the imperial artillery, on getting the news [of their comrade's dishonour], wished to assemble and crowd at the gate of Mirza Tafakhkhur. Aqil Khan, sending the *kotwal*, forbade them. Then he despatched an eunuch of his to Qamar-un-nisa, the daughter of the prime-minister and the mother of Mirza Tafakhkhur, and greatly chid and rebuked him; so that the poor Hindu woman, after the loss of her caste and honour, was given up to the eunuch, and he calmed the artillerymen by promising that a report of the matter would be inserted in the news-letter and the Emperor would certainly remedy [their grievance]. They, therefore, abstained from creating a tumult.

The Emperor, after reading it, wrote across the sheet [of the report], "The prime-minister should write a 'Letter By Order of the Emperor' to Aqil Khan, ordering him to confine in the fort of Delhi this worthless wretch and luckless leader of wicked men; and in case his mother, out of her extreme love for her son, refuses to part with him, the governor [of Delhi] should be ordered to bring Qamar-un-nisa Begam [in] a *chaudol* (rich litter) within the fort with every respect and keep her with her son. Aqil Khan should assign a good house fit for the residence of Qamar-un-nisa Begam. As she is the daughter of my maternal aunt* and is adorned with noble qualities, I ought to show consideration to her internally and externally. But what reform could even the Prophet Noah **(on him and on our Prophet Muhammad be peace!)** make in his own unworthy son, that other [parents] would succeed? It is my duty to prevent oppression on the people, who are a trust from the Creator. Fifty men of the *kotwal* should carefully keep guard round the house and at the gate [of Tafakhkhur's house], so that this noxious creature may not creep out like a snake from a hole. (*Verse*)

Some of these unworthy sons of a Satanic character
Have brought disrepute on some well-reputed [parents]."

The prime-minister at once wrote a 'Letter By Order' and without sealing it placed it before the Emperor with his own letter to Aqil Khan. The

* Ir. MS. has 'my adopted daughter.'

purport of the letter was, "My dear and gracious brother, in view of our longstanding friendship—which dates from the reign of Shah Jahan,—I expect that you would consider yourself as an uncle of the wicked Tafakhkhur. If you send an eunuch, summon him to your presence, and give him fifty stripes with a thorny stick, it will in short give satisfaction and comfort to the loving heart of this brother [of yours]. The thorns of the sticks will extract the thorns planted in my affectionate heart [by my grandson's misdeeds]."

The Emperor after reading it, wrote across the sheet, "Nobody else can chastise the son of my maternal aunt's daughter. If my life lasts and Death grants me respite to return to Delhi, I shall, God willing, chastise him with my own hand. He indeed stands in the relation of a son to me. But what help is there when the son is wicked? **To beat a slave is to insult his master.**" *

*Text.*—Ir. MS. 11*b*—12*b* ; MS. N. 16*a*—18*a*.

*Notes.*—Asad Khan had married one of the four sisters of the Empress Mumtaz Mahal, and he was therefore the maternal uncle of Aurangzib. Many other profligate descendants of Asad Khan are mentioned in *Masir-ul-umara*, i. 320. The confinement of Tafakhkhur is referred to in some of Aurangzib's letters *viz.*, Inayetullah's *Ahkam-i-Alamgiri*, 145*b*, 146*a*, 165*a*, 207*a*, 210*a*, 290*a*. The men of the garrison artillery were taken from the *Baksarias* or Hindu inhabitants of Buxar ; these

---

* In the place of the last sentence, MS. N. gives the following :—

"These dignities that were shown in writing and speaking [about Tafakhkhur] were due to the maxim, 'To beat a slave is to insult his master.' If a well-connected man does such wicked deeds, where can he be put to disgrace ?"

people (now called Bhojpuris) long supplied the E. I. Co. with matchlockmen and the zamindars with clubmen. Aqil Khan (surnamed Razi) was subahdar of Delhi from October, 1680 to his death in 1696. Noah's undutiful son was Canaan. "Noah awoke from his wine, and knew what his younger son had done unto him. And he said, Cursed be Canaan." (*Genesis*, ix. 24).

## § 49. Vigilance against foreign invader's stratagem.

From the news-letter of the province of Afghanistan, the Emperor learnt that eleven thousand horses fit to be cavalry remounts, with one groom for every two horses, had entered Kabul, it being usual that after selection by the governor of Delhi the horses were sent to the Emperor. Across the sheet of the news-letter the Emperor wrote :—"It is a very strange act of negligence on the part of Amir Khan [the governor of Afghanistan] who has been trained by me and knows my mind. It is as if 5,500 brave Turanis have entered the imperial territory from foreign parts. Well, such [was the number of the] men who wrested the kingdom of Hindustan from the hands of the Afghans. However, **a mistake should not be punished and carelessness should not be chastised [like a deliberate sin].***

In future he should know it to be his duty to avoid this sort of action, and he should remedy the past in this way, that whenever the droves of horses arrive [at the frontier], he should allow only one groom to every

* This Arabic passage occurs in MS. N. only, where it is followed by a Persian rendering, with the additional note that the translation formed no part of what Aurangzib wrote.

20 horses, and that groom too should be a useless old and helpless man."

*Text.*—Ir. MS. 5*a* ; MS. N. 34*b*—35*a*.

*Notes.*—Amir Khan (son of Khalilullah) was governor of Afghanistan from 19th March, 1677, to 28th April, 1698, (*Masir-ul-umara,* i. 277). Muhammad-i-Bakhtiar's troopers invading Bengal were not resisted as they were at first imagined to be horse-dealers. (Raverty, 557).

## § 50. Be ever vigilant against foreign Powers.

From the despatch of Amir Khan, the governor of Kabul, it came to the Emperor's knowledge, "It has been learnt from the letter of the *thanahdar* of Ghaznin that the Persian frontier was 36 miles [from Ghaznin], but now the *thanahdar* of that side (*i.e.*, Persia) in the region of Qandahar, says that if we permit him to set up his outpost (*thanah*) four miles further towards our side, every year a hundred Persian horses would be presented to His Majesty. As the water has dried up on the site of the former outpost, and water is available four miles from it [towards the Mughal frontier], he has made this request."

The Emperor wrote in answer, "It is not the part of a wise man to contribute to the vigour and splendour of the Persian *thanahdar* and to rob his own administration of its cover. But, (*verse*)

The word *tam'a* [=greed] has three letters, all of which are empty, [other meaning, 'without dots'].

What do you talk of permitting him to come two *kos* [towards our frontier], when I would not let him come even two steps nearer? It is the opinion of theologians in all religions that persistence in trivial sins is equivalent to committing a mortal sin. I wonder at this hereditary servant, aware of my sentiments,—who has been brought up in my Court from the age of seven years,—being negligent about the devices of the Persians! Consider for yourself why they have consented to present me with a hundred Persian horses, whose price must be high, in return for this simple matter that their outpost might be set up four miles towards our side of the frontier. It is according to that very proverb,—(*verse*)

'He holds the tip of the finger with the design of breaking it,
And then all of a sudden he will attack the arm.
Be not negligent about your enemy's plans,
Always scratch his black face.'

It is a well-known saying (*verse*)

'Wisdom and fortune are closely connected with each other.
He who lacks wisdom, has neither any fortune.'

The common people, who are **like beasts,** imagine that whosoever is a man of fortune must necessarily be a wise man, but it is a wrong idea. The real meaning [of the proverb] is that if a man is not wise his fortune does not last long, and hence we may say that it does not exist. To use more words on this point is like striking an iron when cold, or sewing an old coat."

*Text.*—MS. N. 12*a* 11—13*b* 1.

*Notes.*—Under Shah Jahan and Aurangzib there was the greatest rivalry between the Shah of Persia and the Emperor of Delhi, and several alarms about a Persian invasion of India. Indeed, the Persian peril hung like a dark cloud over certain periods of these two reigns, and our Emperors felt relief on hearing of any warlike Shah's death. Qandahar had been won by the Persians in 1649. [*Hist. of Aur.* iii. ch. 29]. Mir Khan, a son of Khalilullah Khan, was created Amir Khan;

he governed Afghanistan from 19th March, 1677, to his death, 28th April, 1698. (Life in *M. U.* i. 277). See *A Muslim Heroine* in my *Studies.*

## § 51. Promptitude in repelling foreign invasion.

From the news-letter of Persia sent by Muhammad Sadiq, the leader of the merchants, the Emperor learnt that Shah Abbas had left his capital Isfahan, halted two leagues outside the city, and sent his 'advance-tents' on towards Aghrabad. The Emperor immediately mounted his own Arab horse and issued forth. Nobody could venture to speak to him [against this course] at that time. Muhammad Amin Khan, the son of Mir Jumla, being exceedingly bold, submitted, "Your Majesty's 'advance-tents' have not been sent forward yet. It is necessary to halt till they arrive [at the next stage]."

His Majesty answered, "Before I knew [of the Persian king's hostile intentions] I might have been excused [for lingering here]. But after getting the information, negligence and delay would only be causes of the decline of my fortune. What need is there of the arrival of the 'advance-tents ?' (*Verse*)

The man of God is not a stranger in the east or the west;
Whichever way he goes, the country has not parted from Him!"

After entering the garden [outside Agra], the Emperor held a public audience and told his officers and clerks that the march would begin the next day and that he would halt [only on reaching] Lahor. The Chamberlain petitioned, "This march has been undertaken all of a sudden. It is impossible for the necessary things to reach us."

Across the sheet of the petition the Emperor wrote, "The eternal journey, which no man can avoid, will have to be undertaken all of a sudden, without previous warning. What shall I do *then* ? This my present journey should be considered as like that [eternal voyage]. I shall march further on in the same manner in which I have arrived up to this place. Nay, it is not even necessary to mark out the stages [for the successive days' marches]; I shall [daily] travel as far as I can. (*Verse*)

The wayfarer in the path of death is not in need of stages."

*Text*.—Abdus Salam Khan's second MS.

*Notes*.—In September, 1666, Aurangzib, then at Agra, learnt from the reports of his spies that Shah Abbas II wanted to enter Khurasan with a view to invading India. The Emperor at once sent his son Muazzam with Jaswant Singh towards the Panjab (4th September). On 9th October, he himself left Agra for Delhi, but made no haste to reach the north-western frontier. On 12th December, at the hunting-lodge of Palam, he learnt that the Shah had died on 22nd August. (*A. N.* 974, 984 ; *M.A.* 56—58). A taunting letter which the Shah sent to Aurangzib by the hand of Tarbiyat Khan, the Mughal envoy in Persia, shortly before his death, is given in *Faiyaz-ul-qawanin*, 496-499. In it he threatens to invade India. [*History of Aurangzib*, iii. ch. 29].

## § 52. Persians and Indians contrasted.

The Emperor learnt from the news-letter of Ghaznin, "Subhan Quli, the *thanahdar* of the Persian frontier, has written a letter to Amir Khan, the governor of Kabul, saying, 'Between the two frontiers there is a distance of 4 leagues. Praised be God ! friendship and alliance prevail between the two countries ; and there is no apprehension of quarrel and rupture on any account whatever. It is proper that the people of each side should go to the other side for buying and selling, so that both the places may increase in prosperity.' Amir Khan wrote in reply, 'I shall report the point to His Majesty, and inform you of the order that I got.'" The same thing was brought to the Emperor's notice in the report from Kabul.

On the sheet of the news-letter of Ghaznin, Aurangzib wrote, "My reply is written on the report of Kabul,"—which was this : "I wonder that Amir Khan,—a hereditary servant aware of my sentiments, whose ancestors from generation to generation had lived in the society of my ancestors of the house of Timur,—has forgotten the sense of this couplet :

> Don't give up caution when your enemy turns gentle ,
> Stratagems may be concealed under a veil, like water under grass.

Without [being charged with] prejudice and enmity, we may say that as the Sun is the guardian planet of the Persians, the intellectual keenness of those men in quickness of perception and foresight is four times as great as that of the Indians, whose tutelary planet is Saturn. Their only defect is that by reason of its conjunction with Venus, they have grown ease-loving, whereas men governed by Saturn are accustomed to toil ; and the nearness of Saturn to Jupiter is really more frequent [than that of the Sun to Venus ?] But there is a little natural inferiority and meanness in Saturn, the exceptions being certain individuals only, in whose horoscopes some other planet is their helper. The purport of my words is this, that you should be on your guard against the great cunning of the Persians and never submit to me such [seemingly] friendly overtures, as they only prove your lack of sagacity. (*Verse*)

The flood kissed the foot of the wall only to overthrow it !"

*Text.*—MS. N. 29*b* 1—30*b* 5.

## § 53. A Subordinate Officer protected against his Superior.

Jan-nisar Khan, deputy governor of Haidarabad, acting for Ruhullah Khan, petitioned the Emperor thus, "Although this hereditary servant was appointed deputy governor at the request of the chief paymaster, Ruhullah Khan, yet the latter has become a cause of trouble to me without any reason, and wishes to remove me from the deputyship. As the Khan's mind, in the manner of a serpent (*mar*), is always bent on doing harm, I hope that your Majesty will summon this slave to the Presence, so that he may be delivered from these perplexities caused by the worst of men."

Above the word *mar* the Emperor wrote the letter *he*, making it *himar* (= ass), and also "The poor man, whose name has been corrected by adding the letter *he* has no power to do harm [like an ass]. But what remedy is there for a bad nature?"

The contents of the Emperor's writing,—"The deputy [governor]-ship has been conferred at his recommendation. What power has he to dismiss? It is [like] that saying, 'A thief is chained at the words of a peasant, but not released at his request.' If he complains [against you], then, **Whosoever dug a pit for his brother will certainly himself fall into it.** That is,

I shall remove him from the post of paymaster of *tankha*."

*Text.*—MS. N. 4*b* 4—5*a* 3, and then 4*b* 1—4.

*Notes.*—Ruhullah Khan I., Mir Bakhshi, was appointed subahdar of Haidarabad soon after the annexation of the kingdom, 1687. (*M. U.* ii. 313). But he was evidently removed from the post shortly afterwards. Jan-nisar Khan (Khwajah Abul Mukarram, *M. U.* i. 537), was never deputy governor of Haidarabad, but was appointed *diwan* of Bijapur in Feb., 1690 (*M. A.* 328, 335). Ruhullah Khan had been appointed subahdar of Bijapur in Sept., 1686, (*M.A.* 282). There was a Jan-sipar Khan (Mir Bahadur-dil, 3rd son of Mukhtar Khan Sabzawari), who served as governor of Haidarabad for many years after its conquest with great success and credit (*M.U.* i. 536). Probably the scene of the episode was Bijapur. where Jan-nisar Khan served under Ruhullah Khan.

## § 54. Aurangzib's just dealing with his officers.

Yar Ali Beg, the superintendent of the office of the High Diwan, submitted to the Emperor, "By your Majesty's order, whosoever does not get a *jagir* for six months, makes a demand on your Majesty's agent (*wakil*) and takes his cash salary for six months. This order appears to me difficult to carry out. I have, in order to effect a saving to Government, laid it down that they should not demand [their salary] until they get their *jagirs*."

The Emperor wrote, "**First one request, then another.** It is not the act of a wise man to attend to the profits of this perishable world and thereby earn eternal punishment. Wait for a few days, so that, after the close of the utterly dark reign of this man drowned in the ocean of sin and [the commencement of] the times of my foolish sons, the officers will get promissory bonds that their due *jagirs* would not be given to them before the Day of Judgment!" Then he added in slanting lines, "You are the superintendent of the office. Why do you not exert yourself about giving *jagirs* to people, which may be a cause of your good name in this world and of merit in the next life, and which may relieve this rancour-less humble creature [*i. e.*, Aurangzib] of the heavy load of the [unsatisfied] dues [of my officers]? (*Verse*)

Alas, my life has been wasted in vain!
This world has passed away in labour, and
faith has gone out of my hand!
I have angered God, and [yet] not pleased the people,
I have [merely] consumed a quantity of water
and fodder [like a cattle].

Though I am a bad man and know myself to be such, yet, O Great God! save [men] from the greater wickedness than mine that will prevail after my time!"

*Text*—Ir. MS. 17*a* & *b*.

*Notes.*—Yar Ali Beg was appointed assistant *(peshdast)* of the 2nd paymaster in Oct. 1686. He is best known as superintendent of the postal department, and greatly increased the power of the news-writers. (Khafi Khan, ii 410).

## § 55. No money for repairing forts.

Ruhullah Khan II., (whose name was Mir Hasan), petitioned the Emperor, "The fort of Islampuri is weak and your Majesty will soon march [to it]. It requires repair. What order on this point?"

The Emperor wrote, "God pardon us! God pardon us! it was improper for you to write the word 'Islampuri' in a context speaking of 'weakness'. Its old name was Brahmapuri, which you ought to have used. The fort of the body is even weaker than it. What remedy is there for *that*? (*Verse*)

> We have adorned ourselves with works of water and mud:
> We have pampered ourselves instead of preparing our [heavenly] home."

The Khan next urged, "If your Majesty orders it, the Government masons may inspect the fort of Brahmapuri." The Emperor wrote [in reply], "It is a kind of play to you to repeat this request in spite of my former reply. (*Verse*)

> Don't be the architect of your own [self], lest you should ruin the houses.
> Be a ruin, so that on you may be raised a lofty structure.
> Be level with the dust, draw not your neck [back] from anybody.
> It is fitting that the dust should not be raised higher than the ankle of the feet.

If life be yet spared to me and I return, I shall consider the question of repairing [the fort]. If, however, matters end otherwise, what need is there that for [the fulfilment of] the verse, **'Veril youry property and your children are your enemies,'** I should waste the money of the holy warriors [of Islam]?"

*Text.*—Ir. MS. 19*a*, MS. N. 40*b* & 8*a* & *b*.

*Notes.*—Mir Hasan, successively created Khanahzad Khan and Ruhullah Khan II., was the son of Ruhullah Khan I. (Life in *M. U.* ii. 315—317). He was 2nd paymaster and *khan-i-saman* at the time of his death, 9th May, 1704. Aurangzib means that it is an insult to his religion to describe anything bearing the name of *Islam* as weak, hence the old Hindu name of the place, *viz.*, (Brahmapuri) should have been used! His reply throws light on the overwhelming financial difficulties of the last years of the reign.

## § 56. No money for repairing forts.

The letter of Mansur Khan, governor of Aurangabad, was placed before the Emperor. Its purport was, "The imperial camp has reached Ahmadnagar. I consider it necessary to apply for an order for the repair of the citadel of Aurangabad, so that by the time of the arrival of the imperial standards here the repairs may be completed."

The Emperor wrote thus, (*verses*)

"In the grave the earth has opened its arms to receive him,
And the man in his ignorance is painting his house!
It will soon happen that through this negligence, avarice, and desire of his,
His bones and flesh will fall apart from one another!

I wonder at this old servant who knows my feelings making such a request in the face of my order issued on the day of my arrival at Ahmadnagar, 'Write of Ahmadnagar as my **journey's end**.' What chance is there of my going to Aurangabad, when I have spoken of Ahmadnagar as the **terminus of my travels**? In the so many days of my past life there has been no difference (change) in my words! God willing, up to the day of my removal to the eternal home, there will be no difference between my words and acts."

*Texts.*—Ir. MS. 24*a* & *b*, MS. N. 10*b* & 31*a*.

*Notes.*—Aurangzib returned to Ahmadnagar, a broken down old man, ruined in health, finance, and prestige, on 20th January, 1706. (*M. A.* 512). We read of a Mansur Khan, who was superintendent of the Deccan artillery from 1699 to 1705. (*M. A.* 404, 497). A Khwajah Manzur was *qiladar* of Daulatabad in 1658. (*A. N.* 44). The phrase 'journey's end' as applied to Ahmadnagar is given in Khafi Khan, ii. 541, also.

## § 57. Reliance on God in financial difficulty.

Inayetullah Khan submitted to the Emperor, "The retinue (*misl*) of the officers who are daily paraded before your Majesty is unlimited, while the land for granting as *jagirs* is limited. How can an unlimited thing be made to equal a limited one ?"

The Emperor wrote, "God pardon us ! The imperial stores (*karkhanah*) are an emblem of the Court of God. **The people are the children of God and their livelihood is in God's charge.** This poor and humble bread-distributer (*i.e.*, Aurangzib) is no more than an agent of the glorious Lord. To believe that there can be scantiness and limit in God's Court is the essence of infidelity and sin. Praised be God ! and again praised be God ! Although my legs are broken, my heart is not broken. After the capture of Fort Satara *jagir* for 5 or 7 thousands has, according to the statement of Arshad Khan, been added to the dominions of this mortal (= Aurangzib). Make them assignments on this (new territory). When it is exhausted, God will on a new day give you a new source of livelihood."

*Texts.*—Ir. MS. 24*b*.

*Notes.*—Inayetullah Khan (*M. U.* ii. 828) was appointed *diwan of tankha* in July, 1692. He was the "personal disciple" and favourite secretary of Aurangzib, and rose to be *wazir* under Bahadur Shah I. Arshad Khan was appointed *diwan* of *khalsa* in 1698, and died in 1701. *M. U.* i. 290.

## § 58. Mutinous artillery officers cheated.

When the Emperor was marching from Satara towards Fort Parli, the pay of the followers [*ahsham*] and men of the artillery was fourteen months in arrear, owing to the delay in the arrival of the revenue of Bengal. All the four trusted *hazaris* (nominal commanders of one thousand) told the Emperor on the way, "Our followers no longer listen to our words. They want to make an outbreak against Tarbiyat Khan, the chief of the artillery (*Mir Atish*)." His Majesty ordered, "Give them half their due salary from the public treasury inside the harem. For the rest give an assignment on the revenue of Chicacole in the province of Haidarabad, that they may fetch the money thence. Let the prime-minister write a permit to the diwan of Haidarabad and send bailiffs (*sazawals*) with the artillerymen." Man Singh and Chaturbhuj, both of them *hazaris*, did not agree to it, dragged Tarbiyat Khan out of his *palki* during the journey, and made him sit down in the midst of the rain. Yar Ali Beg, the superintendent of the spies (*harkarah*), reported the matter to His Majesty, who immediately ordered the superintendent of the treasury of the harem to pay up their salary in full. They kept the chief of the artillery sitting in this manner in the rain till evening. After they had got their pay, they mounted him [in his *palki*] and brought him to his quarters.

Next morning the Emperor gave robes of honour to each of the four *hazaris* and said, "You have been brought to this [misery] through the wickedness of the chief of the artillery." Tarbiyat Khan's rank was reduced by five hundred, and his *jagir* was decreased to the same extent. After one week he ordered those two *hazaris* to go to Chicacole and draw in advance six months' salary for their comrades. With his own hand he wrote a *farman* to Jan-nasir Khan, the governor [of Haidarabad], ordering him to divide the amount into instalments, and every day pay the instalment due. The news reached the other two *hazaris* who were with the Emperor, and their minds were composed. Then His Majesty ordered that the latter two officers should go to Aurangabad and take from the treasury of that place six months' advance pay for their followers ; and an order was sent to Mamur Khan, the governor of that province, to pay the money by instalments.

After ten days His Majesty ordered that the two *hazaris* who had started first should be confined in the fort of Haidarabad and all the money paid to them, formerly and now, should be taken back ! A similar order was also sent to the governor of Aurangabad, *viz.*, that he should confine (the two men) in the fort of Daulatabad and recover their former and present salaries.

*Text.*—Ir. MS. 23*b* & 24*a*.

*Notes.*—Satara capitulated to Aurangzib on 21st April, 1700, and he marched from it to Parli in three days (28th to 30th April). Mir Muhammad Khalil, (eldest son of Darab Khan of the Mukhtar tribe), was created Tarbiyat Khan and *Mir Atish* about 1698 ; (*M. U.* i. 498—503), died in the battle of Jajau, 1707.

### § 59. Do not provoke a satirical poet.

Kamgar Khan, the son of Jafar Khan, petitioned the Emperor, "Mirza Muhammad Niamat Khan, whose malignant nature is accustomed to satirising, has published certain verses on my marriage, saying, 'The object of it [*i.e.*, marriage] is lawful movement, but in this case there is a coupling of two quiescents.' And he has besides introduced into them other disgraceful remarks about me, so that I have been put to shame before the public. I hope that your Majesty will so punish him that he may not again venture to compose such idle tales. It was proper to submit this matter to your Majesty."

Above the words 'it was proper' Aurangzib wrote 'it was wrong (*haram*),' and on the top of the petition he made this remark, "Punishing him will cause greater disgrace [to you than before]. This simple-minded hereditary servant wishes to make me his sharer in this [public] contempt, so that Niamat Khan may say and write about me whatever [satire] he likes and make me notorious in the world. Formerly, too, he had not spared me [in his satires] ; in return, I had increased his reward, that he might not do it again ; yet in spite of this [favour] he had not on his part been less [satirical]. It is not possible to cut out his tongue and sever his neck. We ought to repress our feelings and live in harmony [with others]. **He is a friend, who neither clings to thee nor separates himself from thee."**

*Text.*—MS. N. 6*b* 7—7*b* 1.

*Notes.*—Kamgar Khan, the son of Aurangzib's early *wazir* Jafar Khan and Farzana Begam, (*M. U.* i. 531) was appointed *khan-i-saman* in 1687, and married the daughter of Sayyid Muzaffar Haidarabadi in September 1688 (*M. A.* 297, 312). Life in *M. U.* iii. 159. His simplicity was notorious. The first couplet of the satire on his marriage is given in *M. U.* iii. 160, and the whole in the *Mazhakat* of Niamat Khan.

Mirza Muhammad Haji Niamat Khan, poetical name Ali, was the son of an eminent Persian doctor, Hakim Fatih-ud-din. Under Bahadur Shah he got the title of Danishmand Khan. He wrote the *Bahadur-Shahnamah*, *Jangnamah*, *Waqai*, and

*Mazhakat*, and was the most famous satirist of the age (*M. U.* ii. 690 : *M. A.* 267 ; Khafi Khan, ii. 338, 359 ; Elliot's *History of India*, vii. 200). There is a play upon the word *quiescent*, which means (1) a consonant not followed by a vowel and therefore incapable of being joined to another letter, and (2) a man wanting in 'virility.

## § 60. A backbiter punished.

From the report of the army of Prince Muhammad Azam Shah, who was then at Ahmadabad, the Emperor learnt that one Muhammad Beg, who was of the prince's troop of *ahadis*, had by means of backbiting secured the prince's companionship and become the cause of harm to many of his servants.

His Majesty wrote, "Siadat Khan should send strong mace-bearers [sergeants] to bring that graceless backbiter—who is the ruiner of the State—to my presence, walking on foot, because the most harmful of all bad things on the part of kings and rich men is the company of backbiters and calumniators. **Mischief-making is worse than murder.** [MS. N. adds]: According to the saying, **'Verily the outside of a snake is many-coloured, but within it there is poison,'** such is the character of a backbiter that externally he looks charming, but at heart he holds a deadly poison. **Avoid him! avoid him!**"

*Text*.—Ir. MS. 19*a* & *b*, MS. N. 9*b*.

*Notes*.—Prince M. Azam was sent to Gujrat, (capital Ahmadabad), as governor in the middle of 1701 and stayed there till 25 Nov. 1705, when he came back to the Court. *Ahadis* were gentlemen troopers, recruited singly, serving the Emperor directly, and not attached to any chief. (Irvine's *Army of the Indian Moghuls*, 43). Siadat Khan IV., the son of

Sayyid Ughlan (Siadat Khan III) was appointed superintendent of "the confirmation of postings" in 1699.

## § 61. Angry Governor punishes his slanderer.

From the letter of Muhammad Azam, news-writer of the province of Gujrat,—who was one of the Emperor's own retainers (*walashahi*), His Majesty learnt that Muhammad Amin Khan, the governor of the province, had held Court while intoxicated with wine. The Emperor wrote [on the sheet]:—"**God is holy! This is a great slander.**" The [Court] agent of Muhammad Amin Khan wrote of this matter to his master. The governor in open *darbar* ordered the moustaches and beard of the news-writer to be pulled out and flung into the air. This, too, reached the Emperor's knowledge. His Majesty wrote:—"His Holiness Ali has said, '**Anger is a sort of madness, and there is no law in madness.**' The Khan has a very violent temper. But in this matter what is known is that the news-writer had calumniated him. What power had he that the smell of wine should reach from the Khan's mouth to his [nostrils]? But, after all, his punishment belonged to me, and it was improper for the governor to inflict it himself. The sentence on the lying news-writer is dismissal from his post, and that on the governor will be withholding from him the robe of honour at the annual [coronation] festival."

*Text.*—Ir. MS. 6*b*—7*a*.

*Notes.*—Muhammad Amin Khan *Hafiz*, son of Mir Jumla, was governor of Gujrat from 11th June, 1672, to his death, 16th June, 1682. A very proud and self-willed nobleman and a bigoted Shia. (Life in *Masir-ul-umara*, iii. 613).

## § 62. Official discipline—both sides punished!

Yar Ali Beg, the superintendent of news (*sawanih*), submitted to the Emperor, "Buzurg Ummed Khan has insulted Abdur Rahim, the news-writer of the province of Bihar, in open audience, and with disgrace turned him out. If no punishment is inflicted [for this], other writers will abstain from writing the truth about occurrences, and become [mere] servants of the provincial governors If your Majesty, too, acts according to [the proverb] 'Bad humour always attacks the weakest limb,' then your slaves are helpless in obeying [your] orders." The Emperor wrote, "This helpless person [*i.e.*, Aurangzib] is himself weak, and he considers all men, high and low alike, to be weak. '**The strong**' is an attribute that belongs only to the pure nature of God. But low persons should never be domineering to high ones. I punish the news-writer with loss of his rank and dismissal, and the provincial governor with a decrease of 500 in his rank (*mansab*) and [a corresponding] change in his *jagir*."

*Text.*—Ir. MS. 8*b*, MS. N. 36*b*—37*b*.

*Notes.*—Buzurg Ummed Khan, a son of Shaista Khan and the conqueror of Chittagong, was subahdar of Bihar from 1683 (?) to July, 1692, and again at the time of his death, 12th Feb. 1695. (Life in *Masir-ul-umara*, i. 453). Another instance of his haughtiness is given in *Masir-ul-umara*, i. 454.

## § 63. Every regulation to be rigidly observed.

Ruhullah Khan II., whose original name was Mir Hasan, had, on account of the Emperor's great intimacy and trust, been raised to the posts of paymaster of *tankha* (salaries) and Chamberlain (*khan-i-saman*). In spite of his having become a Commander of Three

Thousand, he took his own turn of being present as a *khawas*, but stood at the foot of the Court hall. Through the prime-minister Asad Khan he made the following petition, "My rank is that of a Commander of Three Thousand, and Faizullah Khan *sarbari*, the deputy superintendent, is a Commander of Seven Hundred only. If I am appointed *sarbari* and deputy superintendent, it would be conformable to the favour and grace that result from your Majesty's custom of cherishing your servants."

The Emperor ordered, "There is no objection to your being made *sarbari*, provided that you lose both your present posts and get instead the rank of a Commander of Seven Hundred!" Then Asad Khan asked, "But where should he stand?" The Emperor replied, "There is no place higher than his except over my own head." Then His Majesty continued, "If a single rule is disregarded, all the regulations will be destroyed. Though I have not allowed the violation of any rule [of the Court], men have grown so bold that they request me to set rules aside! When this practice becomes widespread, a great difficulty will arise."

*Text.*—Ir. MS. 5*b*—6*a*, MS. N. 32*b*, 11*a*.

*Notes.*—Mir Hasan, the 2nd son of Ruhullah Khan I. *bakhshi*, was created Khanahzad Khan, and in 1697 got the post of *khan-i-saman* and his father's title. Appointed *darogha* of the imperial retinue, 1699. Created 2nd *bakhshi*, Jan. 1701. Died in the fulness of youth, 9th May, 1704. (Life in *Masir-ul-umara*, ii. 315—317).

## § 64. Official etiquette enforced.

From the report of the province of Bengal the Emperor learnt that Ibrahim Khan, the governor, in excess of pomposity and pride, used to hold Court while sitting on a couch (*charpai*), and the qazi and other officers of Canon Law used to sit humbly on the floor. On the sheet of the report the Emperor wrote:—"The prime-minister should write a 'Letter By Order of the Emperor' to the said governor, stating that if he is unable to sit on the ground by reason of any disease, he is excused till his restoration to health, and he should urge his doctors to cure him soon. As the news-writer (*sawanih-nigar*) has risen to a high rank (*mansab*), he is no longer fit to continue as news-writer. Let him be given a promotion in rank of 100 troopers. Write to Ibrahim Khan to find for him a *faujdari* (militia command) within the jurisdiction of his province, so that the latter too may know the test of report-writing against himself by (other) writers. Yar Ali Beg should think about it and recommend some other news-writer, who possesses dignity."

*Text.*—Ir. MS. 5*a* & *b*, MS. N. 35*a* & *b*.

*Notes.*—Ibrahim Khan was governor of Bengal from 1689 to 1697.

## § 65. Royal prerogative infringed.

From the news-letter of Ahmadabad, then governed by Ibrahim Khan, the Emperor learnt that the Khan used to go to the Jama Mosque riding a *palki*. As even the princes could not go [to church] in a *nalki* without the special permission of the Emperor, the news-writers had asked him 'What should we write?' and he had replied 'Write whatever you like.'

On the sheet of the report His Majesty wrote, "Ibrahim Khan is a hereditary servant, aware of my wishes. He has been enrolled among the *amirs* (higher commanders) from the time of Shah Jahan (now in heaven), and can never act contrary to the rules. As he was twice governor of Kashmir, he is used to ride in *jhampans*, which the news-writers here call *palki* from mere resemblance, (in spite of its) difference of shape. Let the prime-minister write to him, 'Why should you do an act which gives a handle to the news-writers [to complain against you]?' The punishment of the news-writer for his wrong conception is that [though] he is retained at his post, his rank is decreased by 50 and his *jagir* reduced to the same extent."

*Text.*—Ir. MS. 18*b* & 19*a*.

*Notes.*—Ibrahim Khan, son of Ali Mardan Khan, was appointed subahdar of Gujrat in 1705, but arrived at Ahmadabad just at the time of Aurangzib's death (Life in *M. U.* i. 295). He had previously governed Kashmir, 1659—1662, 1677—1689, and 1700—1705. During his administration of Bengal (1689—1697) Rahim Khan's rebellion broke out. *Jhampan* or *dandi* is a boat-shaped chair carried on men's shoulders in the hills. *Nalki* is an open *palki* or litter.

## § 66. Ambition of an Abyssinian admiral.

From the news-letter of Machhli-bandar the Emperor learnt that Siddi Yaqut Khan, the *thanahdar* of Danda-Rajpuri, had inserted a petition under his own seal in the news-letter, stating that if the collectorship (*mutasaddi-gari*) of Danda-Rajpuri were conferred on him, he would render far better service than his predecessors in increasing the prosperity of the place and in sending the imperial customs revenue.

Across the sheet of the news-letter the Emperor wrote, "For a long time I have known of this aggressive and self-willed spirit of Siddi Yaqut Khan. [Here the MS. ends abruptly].

*Text.*—MS. N. 30*b* 6—12.

*Notes.*—All the Siddis (Abyssinians) holding charge of Danda-Rajpuri after 1660 bore the title of Yaqut Khan from the Mughal Government, and acted as the Mughal admirals on the Bombay coast. Khafi Khan often narrates their history. (ii. 225—228, 453—454). Danda-Rajpuri is a town on the Bombay coast, n. w. of Mahabaleshwar, and facing the island of Janjira which was the stronghold of the Abyssinians. Machhli-bandar is the modern Masulipatam, near the mouth of the Kistna river on the east coast. One Siddi Yaqut was collector of Danda-Rajpuri in 1702. (*M. A.* 455).

## § 67. A fragment.

The Emperor wrote on the sheet of the application, "Although he is a child, I know him to be a wise child. Probably he made this petition in a state of *sukr* (=intoxication) which is written with the letter *sin* (=*s*) devoid of dots, whereas *shukr* (=gratitude) is written with the letter *shin* (=*sh*) marked with dots—[though] both the words are of the measure of '*qufl*'. For this sort of gratitude, that *shin* does not help in [supplying] the measure (*wazn*) [of the word *qufl*]."

*Text.*—MS. N. 4*a* 7—11. This fragment comes immediately after the text of § 69, but cannot be connected with the latter, as Ruhullah Khan's petition did not contain the word *shukr*.

*Note.*—The Arabic letter for *s* is turned into *sh* by putting three dots over it. *Measure* &c. are terms of Arabic etymology.

## § 68. Be not too proud of your good service.

"Write to Fathullah Khan that his exploits have been known in detail from the despatches, and they have become the cause of his welcome at Court (*mujra*); but he should not turn this risking of his life into the sale of service (*i.e.*, mercenary work), nor should he displease me by displeasing my generals."

*Text.*—Ir. MS. 12*b* & 13*a*. MS. R. gives only the portion from 'he should not turn.' This letter is given in many of the other collections of Aurangzib's letters, and is No. 123 in the lithographed edition of the *Ruqaat-i-Alamgiri*. I think it has got into the *Ahkam* by mistake.

*Notes.*—Mir Muhammad Sadiq, surnamed Fathullah Khan Bahadur Alamgirshahi, distinguished himself at the sieges of Panhala and Khelna, so that the other imperial generals grew jealous of him. Life in *Masir-ul-umara*, iii. 40—47. *History of Aurangzib*, v. ch. 54 for interesting details.

SECTION IV.

## POLICY TOWARDS SHIAS AND HINDUS

### § 69. Sunni refuses to marry Shia's daughter.

RUHULLAH Khan at the time of his death made a will in the presence of Qazi Abdullah. One clause of his will was this: "I am a Sunni, and have withdrawn from the practice of my [Shia] ancestors. Please wed my two daughters to Sunnis." The qazi reported the matter to the Emperor, who wrote, "Hyprocrisy is practised in lifetime; but is a novelty to play the hypocrite on the death-bed! Probably [he has acted so] out of regard for his sons and surviving relatives. This hypocritical step will benefit him only if his sons also assent to it. At all events you ought to act according to his last will. Give his elder daughter to Prince Muhammad Azim and the younger to Siadat Khan, the son of the late Siadat Khan." Next day Siadat Khan submitted, "This hereditary servant is unwilling [to marry Ruhullah Khan's daughter]. How do we know that she too holds the creed of the Sunnis? In case she perseveres in her own faith, what can be done?"

*Text.*—Ir. MS. 10*a* incomplete at beginning. MS N. 4*a* 1—6.

*Notes.*—Ruhullah Khan I., the son of Khalilullah Khan and Hamida Banu, was *bakhshi* or paymaster from January 1680 to his death (about June 1692). In September 1686 he was appointed subahdar of Bijapur in addition. One of his daughters was married to Prince Azim, a son of Bahadur Shah, on 26th June 1692. (Life in *Masir-ul-umara*, ii. 309—315. His death is described in *M.A.* 348; Khafi Khan, ii. 407). The title of Siadat Khan (the younger) was given to the son of Siadat Khan Sayyid Ughlan, in 1698. Khwajah Abdullah (son of M. Sharif) was appointed qazi of the imperial Court in May 1685: died 1698.

## § 70. Ruhullah Khan's death and funeral.

When the Emperor went to visit Ruhullah Khan in his [last] illness, he was insensible. On regaining consciousness he made a *salam* and recited the following couplet:

With what pride will this supplicant leave the world,
As you have come to his head at the time of his giving up the ghost!

The Emperor burst into tears and said, "In no condition whatever should one despair of God's grace. Recovery and hope are not remote from His mercy (*i.e.*, beyond His power). But as death is inevitable to every man, tell me your heart's wish, and I shall certainly grant it." Ruhullah Khan stretched out his hand, rubbed it on His Majesty's feet, and said, "Through the blessing of these feet all my wishes in lifetime were gratified. I now pray for this only that your Majesty may not mind the incompetence of my sons, but keep them under the shadow of your training, appoint those that are fit for any office to that post, and, in the case of those that are incompetent, remember the services of their forefathers."

The Emperor replied, "I agree with all my heart and life." Then the Khan submitted, "Concerning the marriage of my two daughters, I have already sent a petition to your Majesty through the *nazir*, stating that I have been spiritually guided to the Sunni creed, and given up the practices of my [Shia] ancestors, and requesting that both of them may be married to well-born members of the Sunni sect. I now orally pray that your Majesty may order Qazi Muhammad Akram to come and carry out the washing and shrouding of my corpse." The Emperor bowed his head down, smiled, and said, "Verily, love for his children has rendered this man helpless. There is no falling off in your wisdom and power of contrivance. Most probably you have made this plan in the hope that out of respect for the pure soul of a Sunni I shall look graciously at and show kindness to your children. But this plan will succeed only if every one of them too says the same thing (*i.e.*, accepts the Sunni creed). There is no probability at all that they would lay this shame (*i.e.*, apostacy) on themselves. However, I ought to carry out your last will publicly according to the Canon Law." Saying this he repeated a blessing from the Quran (*fatiha*) and came away.

After the Khan's death, the qazi came according to the will of the deceased. One Aqa Beg, a confidential servant of Ruhullah Khan, showed the qazi a letter written by the Khan and sealed with his own seal, which stated, "If at the time of washing and shrouding my body, the qazi comes according to the will of this humble person and the order of the Emperor, Aqa Beg should be appointed the qazi's deputy for doing this work. This poor man does not venture to give trouble to His Holiness the qazi [for this work]. The mere fact of the qazi coming to my house will be the cause of the salvation of this sinner."

This Aqa Beg had outwardly assumed the titles of Aqa and Beg, but he was [really] one of the expert Shia theologians. The qazi had discovered his scholarship from his having often at parties entered into discussions fearlessly and promptly when face to face with learned men. The qazi, on reading the letter, became aware of the real fact of the matter, *viz.*, the invitation of the qazi and the delegation of the work [of washing] to Aqa Beg was a mere form of pleasantry ( *shakl-i-khush-tabai*). So, being displeased, he told Muhammad Ghaus, the news-writer of the qazi's court, to put it at once in a letter and send the letter to the Emperor quickly by means of a slave (*qul*), so that an answer might be brought.

When the sheet of the news-letter was presented to the Emperor, he wrote, "At the time of his death he has cast disgrace on the whole of his past life, and spread a covering over the face of his work. It is not necessary for the qazi to stay there. The late Khan during his lifetime had made deception his characteristic. And at his death, too, he pursued this detestable habit to the end! What concern have I with anybody's faith? Let Jesus follow his own religion and Moses his own. The proposal for the marriage of his daughters to Sunnis was also a kind of stratagem, [employed in the hope] that the poor simple-witted young nobles who would be involved in this misfortune (*i.e.*, would marry these Shia girls) would necessarily, out of love for their wives, withdraw their hands from the long-standing faith of their ancestors and become new converts to Shia-ism. **God protect us from the wickedness of our passions and the sinfulness of our actions.**"

*Text.*—Ir. MS. 13*a*—14*a*; MS. N. 13*b*—16*a*.

## § 71. Hindu prisoners of war executed.

During the siege of the fort of Satara, in the blessed month of Ramzan, four Muslims and nine Hindus out of a party that had made a sortie from the fort, were taken prisoner. The Emperor ordered Qazi Muhammad Akram, the Court Qazi, to investigate the question with the help of the *muftis* and report as to what should be done. After examining [the books of Canon Law], he told the Emperor that if the infidels accepted Muhammadanism it would be a ground for releasing them, and that the Muslims should be kept in prison for three years.

Across the sheet of the legal opinion His Majesty wrote, "This decision [is] according to the Hanafi school; decide the case according to some other school, so that control over the kingdom may not be lost. Ours is not the rigid Shia creed, that there should be only one tree in an entire village.* Praised be God! there are four schools [of Sunni theology] based on truth, [each] according to a particular age and time."

After he had written this, the qazi and *muftis* pronounced another decision, saying, "From the *Fatawa-i-Alamgiri* we derive the sentence that the Hindu and Muslim [prisoners of war] should be executed as a deterrent." The Emperor wrote, "I agree to it. They must be executed before I break the fast [of Ramzan, at sunset], for I shall not break my fast till I have seen the [severed] heads of the rebels." So, Muharram Khan, with the help of Sarbarah Khan *kotwal*, about sunset brought the heads and placed them before the Emperor in the court of justice.

* The reading of MS. N. Its meaning is supplied by Ir. MS. which reads 'that only one decision can be extracted from it.' At the end of this paragraph, MS. N. has two more sentences which do not occur in B.

*Text.*—Ir. MS. 8*a* & *b* ; MS. N. 35*b*—36*b*.

*Notes.*- Satara was captured by Aurangzib after a siege extending from 8th December 1699 to 21st April 1700. The execution of prisoners of war here is noted in the *Akhbarat.* Muhammad Akram was appointed qazi of the imperial Court in May 1698 and died shortly after October 1705. There are four schools of Islamic law accepted by the Sunnis, *viz.*, the Hanafi, the Shafi, the Hanbali, and the Maliki. The *mufti* is an officer who expounds the law and assists the *qazi* or judge by supplying him with *fatawas* or decisions. The *Fatawa-i-Alamgiri* is a code of the decisions of former Islamic lawyers selected, harmonised and arranged by order of Aurangzib, by a syndicate of scholars under the presidency of Shaikh Nizam, at a cost of nearly two *lakhs* of Rupees. It was a mere compilation, with none of the originality and value of the *Code Napoleon.*

## § 72. The Jaziya to be inexorably levied.

The Emperor learnt from the letter of Firuz Jang Khan, who was appointed to take care of the Base Camp (*bungah*) at Islampuri and to guard the road from Burhanpur to the place of the Emperor's stay,—"The tomb of the old slave-girl, the mother of [this] hereditary servant, is on the other side of the river Bhima. It is necessary to increase the population of the grain-market of the place, and thereby ensure the copious arrival of provision at the imperial camp. But this [peopling of the place] cannot be effected without abolishing the poll-tax (*jaziya*) on the Hindu residents of the place. Please order that Inayetullah Khan may send a letter patent (*sanad*) of exemption [from the *jaziya*]."

The Emperor wrote, "**I do not accept helpers from among the infidels.** Your wish for the colonising of the grain-market at the tomb, and your upsetting the command contained in the text of the holy Quran concerning *jaziya*,—which is '**[Chastise them till they pay jaziya from the hand because] they are humbled**', by substituting for it the words '**they deserve to be excused**',—are a thousand stages remote from the perfect wisdom and obedience to the august Religious Law which are possessed by this trusted servant aware of my sentiments. Evidently, a group of your companions, —the habit of which party, more **despicable than sweepers**, is **to create suspicion in the hearts of men**, —have made you blind and go astray, and have, through immature greed, given to this worthless idea a place in your heart which is **receptive of allurements**. How can this old man, stricken in years and experienced in affairs [*i.e.*, Aurangzib], be deceived? (*Verse*)

Go away! and set this trap for some other bird,
As the nest of the Phœnix is built too high."

*Text.*—MS. N. 5*b* 10—6*b* 6.

*Notes.*—Firuz Jang was sent in October 1701 to guard the imperial Base Camp at Islampuri, on the Bhima river. (*M.A.* 445). For Aurangzib's strictness in collecting the *jaziya*, see Khafi Khan, ii. 279, 378; *Akhbarat*, year 38, sheet 232.

## WORKS OF JADUNATH SARKAR

1. **History of Aurangzib**
   Vols. 1 & 2 (in one) 1618–1659, 2nd edition, 612 pp. ... Rs. 5
   Vol. 3, 1659–1681, 2nd ed., .. Rs. 3-8
   Vol. 4, Southern India 1645–1689 .. Rs. 3-8
   Vol. 5, 1689–1707, 504 pp. .. Rs. 4
2. **Shivaji and His Times**, 2nd ed., revised and enlarged, with a fine portrait, ... Rs. 4
3. **Mughal Administration**, 2nd ed., (size more than doubled) 272 pp. ... Rs. 3
4. **Anecdotes of Aurangzib**, 2nd ed., improved Re. 1-8
5. *Ahkam-i-Alamgiri* (Persian text of the *Anecdotes*), 2nd ed., corrected ... Re. 1
6. **Chaitanya**: his life and teachings, 2nd ed., greatly enlarged, with a fine old portrait, Rs. 2
7. **Economics of British India**, 4th ed., enlarged, (1917) ... Rs. 3
8. **Later Mughals** or Successors of Aurangzib, 1707—1739, by W. Irvine, ed. and continued by J. Sarkar, 2 large vols. (with portrait), each ... Rs. 8

—o—

Prof. Qanungo's *Sher Shah*, the standard history of the Pathan genius, ... Rs. 4

*History of the Jats*, Vol. I. (to 1782), with a foreward by J. Sarkar, ... Rs. 3-8

—o—